Asceticism

Ahmad ibn Hanbal

Translated & Comments by Al Reshah

Alreshah.net

Canada

Copyright © 2018-19 by **Alreshah**

All rights reserved. No part of this publication may be reproduced, distributed or transmitted in any form or by any means, without prior written permission.

Alreshah
www.Alreshah.net

Publisher's Note: This is a translation of book without change of meaning as best as the translator could achieve with few comments in the footnote to clarify.
If any error is found, please contact us through our website alreshah.net.

Book Layout © 2017 BookDesignTemplates.com

Excerpts from The Prophetic Biography/ Ibn Kathir. -- 1st ed.
ISBN 978-1-7753942-8-0

The Book is a Translation and reflects the views of the author and not Al Rehash.

Contents

Prophet Mohammad Peace be upon him asceticism 7

Adam asceticism (Peace be upon him)..64

Noah asceticism (Peace be upon him)..69

Ibrahem Al-Khalil asceticism (Peace be upon him)...................72

Joseph asceticism (Peace be upon him).....................................77

Ayyub-Job- asceticism (Peace be upon him) 81

Younus – Jonah- asceticism (Peace be upon him) 87

Moses asceticism (Peace be upon him) 91

Dawud – David- asceticism (Peace be upon him) 111

Soliman Ascetism (Peace be upon him) 123

Loqman Ascetism (Peace be upon him)..............................128

Jesus asceticism (Peace be upon him) 137

• CHAPTER 1 •

Prophet Mohammad Peace be upon him asceticism

In the Name of Allah, the All-Merciful, Most Merciful

Asceticism of the Messenger peace be upon him

Tell us Sheikh Jalil Al-Adl Nasser Al-Din Abu Abdullah Muhammad ibn Yusuf ibn Mohammed ibn Abdullah Al-Damashqi Shafi'i knew the son of Dmashki Al Shafe' read it as we hear in the months of the year eight and seven hundred and it was said to him: Sheikh Imam Al-Theka Taqi Al-Din Abu Muhammad Abdul Rahman ibn Abi Fahim ibn Abdul Rahman Al-Biladi al-Abbasi, Abu al-Qasim Yahya ibn Asaad ibn Yahya ibn Bulesh the merchant, Abu Talib Abd Al-Qadir ibn Mohammed ibn Yousef Al Yousefi narrated. Abu Ali Al-Hasan ibn Ali ibn Al-Mazhab read it in the first month of Rabea Al Awal in the year of four hundred forty-three narrated. Abu Bakr Ahmed ibn Jaafar ibn Hamdan ibn Malik Alkotaiaa narrated:

Narrated Abi-Horaira: The Prophet (ﷺ) said, 'He who goes to the mosque at dawn or dusk (for Salat), Allah prepares a hospitable abode for him in Jannah, every time when he walks to it or comes back from it'.

Narrated Abdullah-Horaira: 'Mention was made to the Messenger of Allah (ﷺ) of a man who slept until morning came. He said: 'That is because Satan urinated in his ears'. *Narrated Alqama:'* I asked 'A'isha (May Allah be pleased with her) saying how was the Messenger of Allah (ﷺ) praying? She said: who amongst you is capable of doing what the Messenger of Allah (ﷺ) did? His act was continuous. *A'ishah said:* The Messenger of Allah (ﷺ) often said while bowing and prostrating himself; 'Glory be to Thee, O Allah, out Lord.' And 'Praise be to Thee, O Allah, forgive me,' Thus interpreting the (command in the Qur'an). *It was narrated that 'Aishah (May Allah be pleased with her) said:* 'The Messenger of Allah

Asceticism - Part 1 -

bought some food from a Jew on credit, and he gave him a shield of his as a pledge'. **Abu Abdullah Al-Jadali narrated:** 'I asked 'Aishah; how was the ethic of the Messenger of Allah when dealing with his family, she said: 'He was the best of all the people in behavior .He was not obscene, nor uttering obscenities, nor screaming in the markets, he would not return an evil with an evil, but rather he was pardoning and forgiving'. *Hisham Ibn Orwa narrated about a man said:* 'I asked 'A'isha, 'What did the Prophet, may Allah bless him and grant him peace, do in his house?' She replied: 'He patched garments and mended sandals, and such things. *Narrated Al-Aswad:* 'I asked Aisha (May Allah be pleased with her) what did the Prophet (ﷺ) use to do at home ?She replied. 'He used to keep himself busy serving his family and when it was time for the prayer, he would get up for prayer'. *Masrouq narrated that 'Aishah said:* 'The Messenger of Allah did not leave behind a Dirham or a Dinar, or a sheep or a camel, and he did not leave any will'. *Ibn 'Abbas narrated that:* The Messenger of Allah ((ﷺ) when he died) left neither a dinar nor a dirham nor a male slave nor a female slave, and his armor was pawned to a Jew for thirty Sa's of barley'. ***Abu Hurairah (May Allah be pleased with him) reported:*** The Messenger of Allah (ﷺ) never found fault with food. If he had inclination to eating it, he would eat; and if he disliked it, he would leave it. **It was narrated that Anas said:** 'The Messenger of Allah said once: 'By the One in Whose Hand is the soul of Muhammad, the family of Muhammad does not have a Sa' of food grains or a Sa' of dates.' And at that time, they were nine households and he had then nine wives.' ***Abu Huraira reported:*** 'I never saw Allah's Messenger (ﷺ) finding fault with food (served to him); if he liked it, he ate it, and if did not like it he kept silent. *It was narrated from Anas* that a Jew invited the Messenger of Allah to a barley bread and rancid oil and the Messenger of Allah accepted his invitation: **Mu'awiya Ibn Kurra narrated:**

'My father told me: we have lived with our prophet (ﷺ) and we have the two-black food, then said: do you know what are the two black things? He said: no. He said: dates and water .

It was narrated that 'Aishah said 'Oh father', she meant 'The Prophet (ﷺ) ' he left the world without having eaten his fill with barley bread'. **It was narrated that 'Aishah said:**

'There would come a month when no bakery was done in any of the households of the family of Muhammad (ﷺ). He said: 'I said Omm Al-mo'minin, what was the Messenger of Allah eating? She said: 'we had some Ansar neighbors- God bless them – they had some milk from which they were sending to the Messenger of Allah (ﷺ). ***Abo Rabah narrated:*** a man entered to The Prophet (ﷺ) while reclining upon a pillow and holding a plate with a bread on it. He said: 'he put the bread on the ground and withdrew the pillow then said: I am only a slave eating what slave is eating and sits like any slave sits. ***Abo Saleh narrated:*** 'The Prophet (ﷺ) was invited to food. Then when he had finished- and once said – when he had eaten thanked God then said: 'no hot food has entered my stomach since such and such a time. ***Garrir Ibn Hazem said:*** 'I heard Al Hassan saying: when the Messenger of Allah (ﷺ) had food, he ordered to leave on the ground and said: I am only a slave eating what slave is eating and sits like any slave sits'. ***Ibn Kassit narrated:*** The Messenger of Allah (ﷺ) brought almond plumule, when he plunged, he said: what is this? They said: it's almond plumule. the Messenger of Allah (ﷺ) said: put it away from me, it's the drink of rich people'. The Messenger of Allah (ﷺ) said when he sent him to Yemen: ' Beware of living prosperously, the slaves of Allah are not of favor'. ***Badil Al Okbaly narrated:*** The sleeves of Messenger of Allah (ﷺ) reached down to his wrists'. ***Ali Ibn Yazid narrated:*** The

Messenger of Allah (ﷺ) saw Al-Alaa Ibn Al-Hadramy a Qatari shirt with long sleeves. He then asked for a knife and cut it from the edges of his fingers'. **Narrated Imran ibn Husayn:** The Prophet (ﷺ) said: I do not ride on purple, or wear a garment dyed with saffron, or wear shirt hemmed with silk. Pointing to the collar of his shirt Al-Hasan (Al-Basri) said: The perfume used by men should have an odour but no color, and the perfume used by women should have a color but no odour'. **Omar ibn Mohajer narrated:** Omar had a house where he sat alone, in this house he never left The Messenger of Allah (ﷺ).

There was a bed with bad woven on it and a bowl in which he drinks water and a jar with a broken head which he uses in making things, and a leather pillow stuffed with palm fiber or velvet, with dust as if these Germanic pieces has dirt from The Messenger of Allah (ﷺ) hair. Then he says: Koraish this is what Allah, the Mighty and Sublime, has honored and cherished you with, takes out of the world what you see'.

Safinah Abu Abdul Rahman said that a man prepared food for Ali ibn Abu Talib and Fatimah (May Allah be pleased with her) said I wish we had invited the Messenger of Allah (ﷺ) and he had eaten with us. They invited him, and when he came, he put his hands on the side-ports of the door, but when he saw the figured curtain which had been put at the end of the house, he went back. So, Fatimah said to Ali: Follow him and see what turned him back. The Messenger of Allah (ﷺ) said: It is not fitting for me or for any Prophet to enter a decorated house'. *It was narrated from 'Abdullah ibn Abi Umamah that Abi Umamah said:* The Messenger of Allah (ﷺ) said: 'Simplicity is part of faith. Simplicity is part of faith. Simplicity is part of faith'. Abdullah said: this is Abo Umamah Al-Harithi, Abdullah said: I asked my father saying: what is simplicity? He said humbleness in cloths.

Abu Hurairah reported: I saw seventy of the people of the Suffah praying in a garment, some of them reached his knees, others below this. If someone bowed, he held it fearing that his private parts appear'. *'Aishah (May Allah be pleased with her) said:* it may has been seen in the garment of one of us then scrape it, and their garments at this time was of wool'. *Anas Ibn Malik reported:* We were with the Messenger of Allah (ﷺ) on a journey. Some of us were fasting and others were not fasting. We got down at a place on a hot day. Most of us had the cloth for shelter. There were also those amongst us who sheltered themselves against the rays of the sun with the help of their hands. Those who were fasting fell down and those who were not fasting got up and pitched tents and watered the mounts.

Thereupon the Messenger of Allah (ﷺ) said: Those who were not fasting have taken away the reward today'. ***It was narrated from Abu Hurairah that:*** The Messenger of Allah (ﷺ) said: 'I seek the forgiveness of Allah and repent to Him one hundred times each day.'

'Abdullah (May Allah be pleased with her) narrated: The Messenger of Allah (ﷺ) said: 'What do I have to do with the world! I am not in the world but as a rider seeking shade under a tree in a summer day, then he leaves it'. ***It was narrated from Abu Hurairah that the Messenger of Allah (ﷺ) said:*** 'O Allah, make the provision of the family of Muhammad sufficient for them'. ***Abu Hurayra narrated the Messenger of Allah (ﷺ) said:*** 'By the One in whose hand my soul is, if you knew what I knew, you would laugh little and weep much'.

Sweid Abu Al-Maali narrated: I heard Anas Ibn Malik saying: I gave the Messenger of Allah (ﷺ) three birds, his servant fed one bird, the next day she brought it. The Messenger of Allah (ﷺ) told her: Haven't I restrained you from reserving something till tomorrow. Allah, the Mighty and Sublime, brings the food for tomorrow'. ***Anas Ibn Malik narrated:*** 'The Messenger of Allah (ﷺ) never ate on a table, nor on small plates, nor did he eat thin bread.' He said: 'I asked Qatadah: 'So what did they eat on?' He said: 'On the leather dining sheets'. *'Abdullah ibn 'Amr ibn Al-'as (May Allah be pleased with him) reported:*

Messenger of Allah (ﷺ) said, 'Successful is the one who enters the fold of Islam and is provided with sustenance which is sufficient for his day's needs, and Allah makes him content with what He has bestowed upon him.'

Fadalah ibn 'Ubaid narrated: I heard the Messenger of Allah (ﷺ) saying: 'Happiness is due to him who is guided to Islam and possesses provision that suffices him for his day and remains content'. ***Narrated Al-Hasan:'*** the food cloth of The Messenger of Allah (ﷺ) was never removed with food on it'.

It was narrated that Ibn 'Umar said: 'The Messenger of Allah (ﷺ) took hold of some part of my body and said: 'O 'Abdullah, be in this world like a stranger, or one who is passing through, and consider yourself as one of the people of the graves'. Abdullah said to me: 'O Mojahid, when you wake up in the morning, then do not concern yourself with the evening, and when you reach the evening, then do not concern yourself with the morning. Take from your life before your death, and from your health before your illness, since indeed Abdullah, you do not know what your name shall be tomorrow'. ***Mohamed Ibn***

Al-Monkader narrated: It was said: 'O Messenger of Allah, Do people of Paradise sleep? He said: Sleep is a brother to death, and people of Paradise do not die'. *Al-Hassan narrated:* 'The Messenger of Allah never ate his fill from meat & bread except with little. Malik said: I did not know what is little and I asked a Bedouin then he said: when he people meet on food and eat it all'. *Masrouq narrated:* 'The Messenger of Allah said: Spend Bilal, and don't be afraid from lowering the abundance . Abu Abel Rahman said again: don't be afraid from the owner of the throne'. **Akramah reported:** 'Abu Bakr (May Allah be pleased with him) said to the Messenger of Allah, 'O Messenger of Allah, you have become old'. He said: 'I have become old from (Surat) Hud, Al-Waqi`ah, and `Amma Yatasa'alun and Idhash-Shamsu Kuwwirat.''

Salim ibn Abdullah narrated: The Messenger of Allah supplicated: O Allah, provide me with two eyes full of tears, and get healed by fear from you before that the tears become blood and morals become pebbles'. *Ja'far Ibn Soliman narrated:* I heard Thabet saying: 'If the family of the Messenger of Allah (ﷺ) is in need of food, he calls his family: O family, pray pray'. *Ibn Omar narrated:* The Messenger of Allah (ﷺ) was saying in his supplication 'O Allah prevent me like baby' means

Asceticism - Part 1 -

the new born'. ***Tawoos narrated:*** The Messenger of Allah (ﷺ) said: The ascetism in life comforts heart and body. The desire for life extends the misery and sadness'. ***Abdullah Ibn Omar narrated:*** The Messenger of Allah (ﷺ) said: The good condition of the first of nation comes with ascetism and certainty, while the last of it perishes with miserliness and hope'. ***Al Hakam narrated:*** The Messenger of Allah (ﷺ) said: 'If the slave shortened in his acts, Allah afflicts him with misery'. ***Al Hassan narrated*** that a man came to the Prophet (ﷺ) and asked: What is the best faith? He said: Patience and generosity'. ***Saad Ibn Malik narrated:*** The Messenger of Allah (ﷺ) said: The best provision is what suffices, and the best saying is what is hidden'. **Abu Umamah narrated that the Messenger of Allah (ﷺ) said:** Allah (mighty and sublime) said: 'Indeed the best of my believers to Me is the one of meager conditions, who has share in Salat, worshipping his Lord well and. He is obscure among the people such that the fingers are not pointed towards him. His provisions are only what is sufficient, and he is patient with that. Then his death comes quickly, his mourners are few, and his inheritance is little'. I asked my father: 'What is his inheritance?' He said: 'It's his heritage'. ***Mahmoud Ibn Labib narrated:*** The Messenger of

Allah (ﷺ) said:' Allah (mighty and sublime) protects his believer slave and he loves him, as you protect your patients from food and drink as you care about them'. **Qatadah ibn An-Nu'man narrated that the Messenger of Allah (ﷺ) said:** 'When Allah loves a slave, He prevents him from the world, just as one of you prevents his sick from water'. **Mutarrif reported from his father** that he went to the Prophet (ﷺ) and he was reciting: 'The mutual rivalry (for piling up worldly things) diverts you.' He said: 'The son of Adam says: 'My wealth, and do you own anything except what you eat, such that you've finished it, or you wear, such that you've worn it out, or what you give in charity, such that you've spent it'. **'Abd al-Rahman al-Hubuli reported:**

I heard that a person asked 'Abdullah ibn Amr ibn Al-Aas saying: Are we not amongst the destitute of the emigrants? Abdullah said to him: Have you a spouse with whom you live? He said: Yes. Abdullah asked: Do you not have a home in which you reside? The man replied 'Yes.' Abdullah said: Then you are not amongst the destitute of the emigrants. ***Ayoub Ibn Abd Rabu Ibn Sa'eed El-Madany narrated:*** The Messenger of Allah (ﷺ) entered to Othman Ibn Math'oon when dying, then he kissed him and said: 'May Allah put mercy on you Othman! You did not enjoy life and life did not enjoy you'. **Musab ibn**

Asceticism - Part 1 -

Sad narrated: The Prophet (ﷺ) said, 'Beware of life, it is sweet and green'. ***Uqbah ibn Amir reported:*** The Messenger of Allah, peace and blessings be upon him, said: 'if you notice that Allah gives his slave from life what he deserves despite his since, be assured this is just an attraction'. Then he recited the saying of Allah: 'So when they forgot that by which they had been reminded, we opened to them the doors of every [good] thing until, when they rejoiced in that which they were given, we seized them suddenly, and they were [then] in despair'.
'Abdullah narrated:

'The Messenger of Allah (ﷺ) was sleeping upon a mat, then he stood, and the mat had left marks on his side. We said: 'O Messenger of Allah! We said: 'O Messenger of Allah! We could get a bed for you.' He said: 'What do I have to do with the world! I am not in the world but as a rider seeking shade under a tree, then he catches his breath and leaves it'. ***Al-Hassan narrated:*** 'The Messenger of Allah (ﷺ) said: 'Three things not causing a slave to be called to account: a shadow to take as his shelter, a piece to pull his body, and a cloth to cover therewith his private parts'. ***Bayan narrated:*** I was reported that in Tawrah it's mentioned: 'Son of Adam small piece shall suffice you, a piece of cloth shall cover you, and a stone shall be your home'. ***Salem Ibn Abi Al-Ja'ed narrated:*** 'The Messenger of Allah (ﷺ) said: 'It is from my nation who came to someone's door and asked him dinar and did not give him, or dirham and did not give him, or a penny and did not give him. If he asked God for Paradise, he would give it to him, however if he asked God for life, he would not give it to him. He did not take it away from because He did not care about him, an obeying slave does not pay attention to him, if he swore to God, He would have honored him'. **Mohareb Ibn Dathar narrated:** 'The Messenger of Allah (ﷺ) said: 'It is from my nation who cannot come from his mosque or his prayer from the nudity, which his faith holds to ask people, including Awis al-Qarni and Furat ibn Hayyan Al-Ajli'. **Anas Reported:** 'The Messenger of Allah (ﷺ) said: 'The Prophet (ﷺ) said, 'Shall I inform you about the people of Paradise? They comprise every obscure unimportant humble person, and if he takes Allah's Oath that he will do that thing, Allah will fulfill his oath (by doing that)'. ***Abi Al Jawzaa reported:*** 'The Messenger of Allah (ﷺ) said:' Shall I inform you about the people of Paradise and the people of Hell? 'The people of Paradise are those whose ears Allah fills with the bad praise of people when they are listening'. **It was narrated that 'Ali, may Allah be pleased with him, said:**

'The Messenger of Allah fitted out Fatimah with a velvet dress, a water-skin and a leather pillow stuffed with palm fibers .

Asceticism - Part 1 -

Al Hassan narrated: 'Allah's Messenger (ﷺ) bed was of garment and knitted pillow stuffed with palm fibers'. *Akramah Ibn Abbas narrated* that the 'Omar Ibn Khattab (**may Allah be pleased with him**) entered to The Messenger of Allah (ﷺ) when he was upon a mat, then he stood, and the mat had left marks on his side. He said: 'O Messenger of Allah! Why did not you get another bed? '. He said: 'What do I have to do with the world! I am not in the world but as a rider seeking shade under a tree in a summer day, then he catches his breath and leaves it'. *Abdullah Ibn Shaddad narrated the following Hadith:* 'Who wears wool, and arrested the sheep, and riding a donkey, and answered the invitation of the humiliated man or slave, nothing from arrogance would be referred to him'. *Al Hassan narrated:*

'The Messenger of Allah (ﷺ) was praying in his wives' clothes, and their clothes were made of wool, with flags of wool of six dirhams or seven'. *Ismail Ibn Omaya narrated:* 'Aishah (May Allah be pleased with her) made two beddings for The Prophet (ﷺ), but he refused to sleep except on only one'.

Masrooq narrated that 'Aishah (May Allah be pleased with her) reported: 'A woman of the Ansar entered and saw the garment of the Messenger of Allah - peace be upon him – a folded cloak, then she returned to her house and sent me a garment stuffed with palm fibers. I entered to the Messenger of

Allah - peace be upon him – he said: What is this? I said: this Ansari woman entered and saw your bed. He said: return it back to her, then Ii did not return it. I liked to put in my house, until he said this to me three times: O 'Aisha, return it back, I swear to God, if I wish God will grant me mountains of gold and silver. Then I returned it'. **It was narrated that 'Aishah said:** 'The Messenger of Allah (ﷺ) said to me: 'O 'Aishah, beware of (evil) deeds that are regarded as insignificant, for they have a pursuer from Allah'. ***Abdullah ibn Masud narrated:*** 'The Messenger of Allah (ﷺ) said: 'beware of (evil) deeds that gather on a man until they destroy him. Then, the Messenger of Allah (ﷺ) gave them an example of some people came down to a wild land ‹then the best man in them came and he let him to go, and bring the lute, and the man came with the lute, until they gathered black, and they made fire, and they cooked what they threw'. **Abu Hurairah narrated that the Messenger of Allah** (ﷺ) **said:** 'Indeed a man may utter a statement which he does not see any harm in, but for which he will fall seventy autumns in the Fire'. ***Alqama ibn Bilal ibn Al-Harith Al-Muzani (May Allah be pleased with him) reported:*** 'The Messenger of Allah (ﷺ) said, 'A man speaks a good word without knowing its worth, Allah records for him His Good Pleasure till the day he will meet Him; and a man utters an evil word without realizing its importance, Allah records for him His displeasure till the day he will meet Him.' He said, 'Alqama said,' A lot of Bilal ibn al-Harith's speech had stopped me'. ***Uqbah ibn 'Amir narrated:*** 'I said: 'O Messenger of Allah! What is the meaning to salvation?' He said: 'That you control your tongue, your house suffices you, and cry over your sins'. **Jabir ibn Samurah narrated:** 'When the Prophet prayed Fajr he would remain seated where he had prayed until the sun had risen'. *Narrated Ibn Abbas:* 'The Messenger of Allah (ﷺ) said: 'Beware of Prayer at night even for one rak'ah'. ***Fatima (May Allah be pleased with her) narrated:*** 'O Anas! Do you feel pleased to throw earth over Allah's Messenger (ﷺ)?' He said:' Fatima said: O my father, how much closer he is now to his Lord; O my father, the Paradise of Firdaws is his abode; O father! We announce to Jibril your death.' Or she said: 'I announce …' Abo Kamel doubted, O my father, he has answered the call of his Lord'. ***It was narrated that 'Aishah said:*** 'The Messenger of Allah was wearing two thick and rough Qatari garments. She said' O the Messenger of Allah, those two garments are thick and rough, when you put on them, they become heavy on you'. He sent to someone who had cloths from Al-Sham and bought from him two garments on pay-as-you-go basis. He sent to him and said:

'The Messenger of Allah ask you to sell him two garments on pay-as-you-go basis. He said: 'I know what Muhammad wants; he wants to go away with my money and take them (the two garments).' The Messenger of Allah said; 'He is lying; he knows that I am one who fear Allah the most and are most honest in fulfilling trusts'. **Narrated Jabir ibn Abdullah:** The Prophet (ﷺ) said: tell others the stories of Bani Israel, there is no harm, they are weird people'. Then he narrated that (ﷺ) said:

'A group of Bani Israel came out until they came to a grave from their graves. They said: If we prayed two rak'ahs and called upon God to bring us back a man who had died to ask him about death, he said: they did. As of then, a man bring out his head from the grave of those graves, mulatto, between his eyes the effect of prostration, he said: O people, what you wanted for me? I had died since a hundred years, the heat of death hasn't yet calmed down until now, so pray to God Almighty to return me back to the place I were'. **Abu Huraira reported:**

'The Messenger of Allah (ﷺ) said: 'increase your mention of the destructor of pleasures.'

Sofian praised saying: 'Someone praised on The Prophet (ﷺ) and said:' How he mentioned death?' They said: 'it's like this'. He said: 'He is like what you describe'. **Abi Thor**

Asceticism - Part 1 -

narrated: 'The Messenger of Allah (ﷺ) repeated this Ayah until he wakes up: 'If Thou dost punish them, they are Thy servant: If Thou dost forgive them, Thou art the Exalted in power, the Wise'.

Abo Saleh narrated: 'The Messenger of Allah (ﷺ) performed so many prayers that his legs swelled. Someone said to him, God has forgiven your past and present sins? He replied: 'Should I not be grateful servant'.

Abo Saleh narrated: 'I asked 'Aishah and Om Salama: what is the most beloved action to Allah's Messenger (ﷺ)? She said: what is continuous even if it's few.'

Anas Ibn Malik narrated: 'The servant used to hold the Messenger of Allah (ﷺ), he helped her in performing what she needs, and he does not come back until he fulfills what she needs'. ***Hisham Ibn Hassan narrated:*** My father reported me about 'Aishah (May Allah be pleased with her) that: The Prophet (ﷺ) came in when a woman was sitting beside her, and I mentioned she is the one whose performance of Salat (prayer) has become the talk of the town.' Addressing her, he

(ﷺ) said, '(What is this!) You are required to take upon yourselves only what you can carry out easily. By Allah, Allah does not withhold His Mercy and forgiveness of you until you neglect and give up (good works). Allah likes the deeds best which a worshipper can carry out constantly'. ***'Umar (May Allah be pleased with him) said:*** I heard Messenger of Allah (ﷺ) saying: 'If you all depend on Allah with due reliance, He would certainly give you provision as He gives it to birds who go forth hungry in the morning and return with full belly at dusk'. ***Abu Hurairah (May Allah be pleased with him) narrated that the Messenger of Allah (ﷺ) said:*** 'Look at those who are lower than you (financially) but do not look at those who are higher than you, lest you belittle the favors Allah conferred upon you'. ***Abu Hurairah (May Allah be pleased with him) reported:*** The Prophet (ﷺ) said, 'Richness is not the abundance of wealth, rather it is self-sufficiency'.

Ali narrated that the Messenger of Allah said: 'Indeed in Paradise there are chambers, whose outside can be seen from their inside, and their inside can be seen from their outside.' A Bedouin stood and said : 'Who are they for, O Messenger of Allah?' He said: 'For those who speak well, feed others, fast regularly, and perform salat [for Allah] during the night while the people sleep'. ***Abu Hurairah (May Allah be pleased with him) reported:*** the Messenger of Allah (ﷺ) said, 'Do you know who the bankrupt is?' They said: 'The bankrupt among us is one who has neither money with him nor any property'. He said, 'The real bankrupt of my Ummah would be he who would come on the Day of Resurrection with Salat, Saum and Sadaqah (charity), (but he will find himself bankrupt on that day as he will have exhausted the good deeds) because he reviled others, brought calumny against others, unlawfully devoured the wealth of others, shed the blood of others and beat others; so his good deeds would be credited to the account of those (who suffered at his hand). If his good deeds fall short to clear the account, their sins would be entered in his account and he would be thrown in the (Hell) Fire'. ***Narrated Jabir ibn 'Abdullah:*** The sun never rose except with the two angels calling and hearing the people of the earth but the human beings and Thaqlin: O people, come to your Lord, the less and enough is better than many and delude. The sun never went down except with the two angels calling and hearing the people of the earth but the human beings and Thaqlin: O Allah! Compensate to the person who gives (in charity) and destroy the one who withholds (charity)'. ***Abi'l-Hudhayl narrated:*** One of my friends praised about The Prophet (ﷺ) saying: Perish gold and silver, what is your order to us? What should we do? He said: 'a thankful heart, a tongue that remembers Allah and a believing wife who will help him with regard to the Hereafter.' '

'Abdullah ibn 'Amr ibn Al-'As narrated that the Messenger of Allah said:

'If a pellet like this one, and he pointed to one like Al-jumjumah was to be dropped from the heavens to the earth – and it is the distance of traveling for five hundred years, it would reach the earth before the night-fall. But if it were dropped from the top of the chain it would travel for forty years, day and night, before it would reach its foundation or bottom'. **Narrated Abu Sa'eed Al-Khudri:** the Prophet (ﷺ) said: 'Therein they will grin, with displaced lips' he said: 'He will be broiled by the Fire, such that his upper lip will shrink until it reaches the middle of his head, and his lower lip will droop until it is near his navel'.

Abu Hurairah narrated that the Prophet (ﷺ) said: 'Indeed Hamim will be poured over their heads. The Hamim will penetrate until it finds its way to his insides. Then whatever is inside him will fall out until it pours over his feet while it melts away. Then he will be reformed to how he was'. **Abu Umamah narrated regarding His (Allah's) statement:**

'He will be given water of Sadid to drink, he will swallow it...' that the Prophet (s.a.w) said: ' It will be brought toward his mouth and he will dislike it, so whenever it is brought closer to him it will melt his face and the skin of his head will fall into it. Then whenever he drinks from ithis bowels will be severed until it comes out from his anus. Allah, the Blessed and Exalted says: 'And they will be given water of Hamim to drink such that it cuts up their bowels...' and He says: 'And if they call for drink, they will be given water of Muhl which melts the faces, the worst of drinks and the worst of abodes'. *Abo Hazem narrated: I heard Sahl ibn Sa'd As-Sa'idi saying:* The Messenger of Allah (ﷺ) said, 'Verily! Setting out in the early morning or in the evening in order to fight in Allah's way is better than the world and what it contains'. *Al-Bara' ibn 'Azib (May Allah be pleased with them) reported:*

The Messenger of Allah (ﷺ) commanded us to do seven things: to visit the sick, to follow the funeral (of a dead believer) .*Na'im Ibn Hammad narrated:* Messenger of Allah (ﷺ) said that that Allah, the Mighty and Sublime, 'Son of Adam: Perform four Rak'ah for Me in the beginning of the day it will suffice you for the latter part of it'. **Narrated Abu Huraira:**

Allah's Messenger (ﷺ) said, 'The angels keep on asking Allah's forgiveness for anyone of you, as long as he is at his Musalla (praying place) and he does not pass wind (Hadath). They say, 'O Allah! Forgive him, O Allah! be Merciful to him'.

Abo Imama narrated: Allah's Messenger (ﷺ) said : 'who wipes the head of an orphan he had from every hair that passed his hand on it virtues. And who is charitable to an orphan will be in Jannah with me like these two', and he put together his forefinger and middle finger'. ***'Uthman ibn 'Affan (May Allah be pleased with him) reported:*** The Prophet (ﷺ) said, 'There is no right for the son of Adam except in these things: A house to live in, a cloth to cover therewith his private parts, bread and water'. ***Nu'maan ibn Bashir Radiyallahu 'Anhu says:***

'Are you not in the luxuries of eating and drinking. Whereas I have seen your prophet (ﷺ) not having ordinary types of dates to full his stomach'. ***An-Nu'man ibn Bashir narrated:***

I heard the Messenger of Allah - peace be upon him – when he is on the pulpit says: I warn you from hell, until one of the two of his garments fell off his shoulders and said, 'I warn you from hell.' So that if my place to make the people in the market hear me or who wishes that from them and he (An-Nu'man ibn Bashir) is on the pulpit of Kufa. ***Gaber narrated:*** I heard the

Asceticism - Part 1 -

Messenger of Allah (ﷺ) saying: 'Do not wish to die, it frightens the one who witnesses it so much, but it a pleasure for any slave to have long life and be granted with delegation'. ***Narrated Abo Huraira:*** Allah's Messenger (ﷺ) said, 'A place in Paradise equal to the size of a lash is better than the whole world and whatever is in it'. ***Yazid Ibn Abdullah narrated:*** 'If the scholars have kept their learning and deliver it to who deserve, they would dominate the whole people in their life, however they gave it to people who care only about life, then they did not take it seriously'. 'I heard your Prophet (ﷺ) say: 'Whoever focuses all his concerns on one thing, the Hereafter, Allah will relieve him of worldly concerns, but whoever has disparate concerns scattered among a number of worldly issues, Allah will not care in which of its valleys he died'. ***Abu Musa reported Allah's Messenger (ﷺ) as saying:***

Allah, the Exalted and Glorious, grants respite to the oppressor. But when He lays Hand upon him, He does not then let him off. Re (the Holy Prophet) then recited this verse:' Such is the chastisement of thy Lord when He chastises the towns (inhabited by) wrongdoing persons. Surely, His punishment is painful, severe'. ***Narrated Abo Huraira:*** Some of mighty and arrogant men come in the form of tiny insects, overthrown by people due to God's humiliation to them until end of life. He said: 'Then He brings them to the fire of Mighty'. It was said: 'what do you mean by fire of Mighty?'. He said: 'The output of people of Hell'. **Anas narrated:** Allah's Messenger (ﷺ) passed with his friends by a dead lamb. The Messenger of Allah (ﷺ) said: 'Do you think that this was insignificant to its owners when they threw it away?' *It was narrated from Umm Habibah, the wife of the Prophet (ﷺ), that the Prophet (ﷺ) said:* 'The words of the son of Adam count against him, not for him, except what is good and forbidding what is evil, and remembering Allah.' A man said to Sophian: 'How fierce this speech!'. Sophian said: 'Why is it fierce?'. He said: Allah, the Mighty and Sublime, said: 'In most of their secret talks there is no good: But if one exhorts to a deed of charity or justice or conciliation between men, (Secrecy is permissible)'. Allah, the Mighty and Sublime, also said: 'charge one another with the truth and charge one another with patience'. Allah, the Mighty and Sublime, also said: 'they cannot intercede except for him whom He accepted'. Allah, the Mighty and Sublime, also said: 'except any who is permitted by (Allah) Most Gracious, and He will say what is right'. Abo Sophian said: 'this is Allah sayings which Gebra'eh Alayh Al salam came with'. **Anas ibn Malik said :**The Prophet, may Allah bless him and grant him peace, was the most merciful of people towards little kids. He had a

Asceticism - Part 1 -

new born in Madina and the husband of his wet-nurse was a blacksmith. He used to go to him while the house would be full of smoke from the bellows. He would kiss the child and take him in his lap, then comes back'. *Abu Hurairah (May Allah be pleased with him) reported:* The Messenger of Allah (ﷺ) said, 'The best month for observing Saum (fasting) after Ramadan is Muharram, and the best Salat after the prescribed Salat is Salat at night'. *Abu Huraira reported Allah's Messenger (ﷺ) as saying:*

'Those persons who assemble in the house among the houses of Allah (mosques) and recite the Book of Allah and they learn and teach the Qur'an (among themselves) there would descend upon them tranquility and mercy would cover them and the angels would surround them and Allah mentions them in the presence of those near Him, and whoever follows a path in the pursuit of knowledge, Allah will make easy for him a path to Paradise'. *'A'ishah, wife of the prophet (May peace be upon him), said:* I never saw the Messenger of Allah (May peace be upon him) laugh fully to such an extent that I could see his uvula. He would only smile, and when he saw clouds or wind, his face showed signs (of fear). I asked him: Messenger of Allah! When the people see the cloud, they rejoice, hoping for that it may contain rain, and I notice that when you see it, (the signs of) abomination on your face. He replied: 'A'ishah! What gives me safety from the fact that it might contain punishment? A people were punished by the wind. When those people saw the punishment, they said: this is a cloud which would give us rain'. **Anas ibn Malik (May Allah be pleased with him) reported:** *the* Messenger of Allah (ﷺ) said, ' A person who had led the most luxurious life in this world will be brought up on the Day of Resurrection and Allah says: 'dip him in the Fire'. He said: 'they dip him in the fire and he says : 'O son of Adam! Did you ever experience any comfort? Did you happen to get any luxury? Did you feel joyful?' He will reply: O Allah, no.' He says' return him to hell'.

And then one of the people who had experienced extreme misery in the life of this world and was very exhausted' Allah, the Mighty and Sublime, says: 'Dip him in Jannah. Then he will be dipped in Jannah and got it. Then it was said: 'O son of Adam! Did you ever experience anything that you hated? He will say: 'O Allah, no, I never experienced something I hated'. **Umar ibn al-Khattab narrated:** 'The Messenger of Allah, may Allah bless him and grant him peace, said, 'Why did you return it?' He said, 'O Messenger of Allah, didn't you tell us that it is better for us not to ask anything from anyone?' He said, 'That is by asking. Provision which Allah gives you is different from what you ask for'. **Osama Ibn Yazid narrated that the**

Asceticism - Part 1 -

Messenger Of Allah (ﷺ) said: 'I looked into Paradise and I saw that the most of its people were the poor; and I looked into the Fire and I saw that most of its people were women. The wealthy were kept confined. The inmates of the Fire had been ordered to (enter) the Fire (Hell)'. ***It was narrated from Anas that the Prophet (ﷺ) entered upon a young man who was dying and said:*** 'How do you feel?' He said: 'I have hope in Allah, O Messenger of Allah, but I fear my sins.' The Messenger of Allah (ﷺ) said: 'These two things (hope and fear) do not coexist in the heart of a person in a situation like this, but Allah will give him that which he hopes for and keep him safe from that which he fears'. ***Anas said:***

'A man came to the Messenger of Allah (ﷺ) and said: 'I intend to undertake a journey, so give me provision. He said: 'May Allah grant you Taqwa as your provision'. He said: 'Give me more.' He said: 'And may He forgive your sin'. He said: 'Give me more, may my father be ransomed for you, and my mother.' He said: 'And may He make goodness easy for you wherever you are'. ***Narrated Anas ibn Malik:*** the Messenger of Allah (ﷺ) said: 'How many are there with dishevelled hair, covered with dust, possessing two cloths, whom no one pays any mind to - if he swears by Allah then He shall fulfill it.

Among them is Al-Bara ibn Ma'ror, may Allah be pleased with him'. ***Abu Burda reported:*** A'isha brought out for us the coarse lower garment (of Allah's Messenger) made in Yemen and clothes made out of Mulabbada cloth, and she said that Allah's Messenger (ﷺ) died in these two garments. ***Talha Al-Basri narrated:*** I came to Madina and I did not know anything about it, and we get dates. The Messenger of Allah (ﷺ) prayed with us when something called from inside him, then he said: O Messenger of Allah, our stomach was burnt by dates and our cloth were torn. When Messenger of Allah (ﷺ) finished Salah, orated and thanked Allah then he said:" By Allah, if I find meat and bread, I will feed you with, and one day you will feed each other with bowls, and will dress like Ka'bah curtains. They said: today is better or that day? He said: Today is better as on that day you will be cutting the necks of one another. ***Anas ibn Malik narrated:*** The Messenger of Allah (ﷺ) sent to a jew asking to borrow something on pau-as-you-go basis. The Jewish said: Is it true that Mohamed will pay for it later? He said: I came to Mohamed and informed him, he said: The Jewish lied three times, I am the best who sold things three times, it's better for a man to wear a cloth with many patches than to take what he does not own'. ***Thawban narrated:*** 'When (the following) was revealed: And those who hoard up gold and silver' He said:

Asceticism - Part 1 -

'We were with the Messenger of Allah (ﷺ) during one of his journeys, so some of his Companions said: (This) has been revealed about gold and silver, if we knew which wealth was better than we would use it. So, he (ﷺ) said: 'The most virtuous of it is a remembering tongue, a grateful heart, and a believing wife that helps him with his faith'.

Attaa Ibn Yasar narrated that the Messenger of Allah sent Moath to Yemen and he said: 'O Messenger of Allah, tell me what to do. He said: You have to fear God as much as you can, and remember Allah at every stone and tree, and what if you commit bad action, perform the repentance of secret by secret and openness by openness'. ***Abu Hurairah (RAA) narrated that the Messenger of Allah (ﷺ) said:*** 'If people sit in an assembly in which they do not remember Allah or invoke blessings on the Prophet it will be a cause of grief to them on the Day of Resurrection'. **It was narrated that Abu Dharr narrated that he asked** Messenger of Allaah to advise him. He said:' If you do bad deeds, then follow them with good ones that remove them.' I said: 'is it a virtue to confess that no God but Allah'. He said:' it's the best virtues ever'. ***Abo Al Garah narrated*** that a man from his companions called Khazem told them that Gebr'el (peace be upon him) came to the Messenger of Allah (ﷺ) when he was sitting with a man crying, he said: who is this? He said: someone. Gebre'l said: we weigh all the acts of the son of Adam except crying, Allah, the Mighty and Sublime, turn down the Hell fire by tears. **Rabah narrated:** the Messenger of Allah (ﷺ) said to Gebr'el (peace be upon him): I never saw you except with a sadness in your eyes. He said:" I haven't laughed since the fire was created'. **Anas Ibn Malik narrated:** I heard The Messenger of Allah (ﷺ) saying: 'If you know what I know, you will laugh a little and weep a lot. ***Abu Duhr (may Allah be pleased with him) narrated:*** The Messenger of Allah (ﷺ) told me: O Abo Duhr, look at the top man in this gathering. He said: I looked then saw a man with a suit. He said: I said" that man" He said: look at the lowest man in this gathering". He said: I looked at a man with morals". He said: that man". The Messenger of Allah (ﷺ) said" this man is better to God in the Day of Resurrection than all what in this life'. ***Abu Hurairah (May allah be pleased with him) reported:*** Messenger of Allah (ﷺ) said: 'The world is the believer's prison and the infidel's Jannah'. ***Abo Duhr narrated:*** A man came to the Messenger of Allah and said: 'O Messenger of Allah we have been eaten by hyenas. He said: there is another thing that fears me about you, this world will come to you in plenty. I wish my people don't wear gold. I said to Yazid ibn Wahab: 'What is hyenas?'. He said: 'dryness'. **Mohamed ibn Monkader narrated:** The Messenger of Allah (ﷺ) said, "The world, with all that it contains, is accursed except what is for Allah, the Mighty and Sublime'. **Abdullah [ibn Mas'ud] narrated** that the Messenger of Allah (ﷺ) said: 'Do not take to the estate, such that you become desirous of the world'. **Abdullah ibn Umar narrated:** 'The Messenger of Allah(ﷺ) came upon us when we were repairing our cottage that was broken. He asked: What is this? We replied: This cottage of ours has broken and we are repairing it. The Messenger of Allah(ﷺ) said: I see that the command is quicker than that'.

Ibn 'Abbas reported: The Messenger of Allah (ﷺ) went to bed hungry for several successive nights, nor did his family have a thing for supper for many consecutive nights; and their bread was mostly of barley.' Abo Sa'eed said: 'their food was mostly of barley'. **Simak b. Barb reported:** I heard Nu'man (Ibn Bashir) deliver an address saying: Umar made a mention of what had fallen to the lot of people out of the material world and he said: I saw Allah's Messenger (ﷺ) spend the whole day being upset because of hunger and he could not get even an interior quality of dates with which he could fill his belly. **Aishah (May Allah**

be pleased with her) reported: The family of Muhammad (ﷺ) never ate to the fill the bread of barley for two successive days until he died. ***It was narrated that Mu'adh ibn Jabal said:*** 'Their sides forsake their beds, to invoke their God in fear and hope'. He said:' the slave wakes at night'. ***Abu Umaamah Al-Baahili Radiyallahu 'Anhu says:*** 'Bread made of barley was never left over in the house of the prophet (ﷺ)'. ***Abo Kelaba narrated:*** The Messenger of Allah(ﷺ) said: 'the Then on that Day, you shall be asked about the delights!' He said: 'People of my nation are mixing ghee and honey then eat it. **Abu Hurairah narrated that :** the Messenger of Allah said: 'Indeed the first of what will be asked about on the Day of Judgment – meaning the slave (of Allah) being questioned about the favors – is that it will be said to him: 'Did We not make your body, health, and give you of cool water to drink? ***Mutarrif reported on the authority of his father:*** that he went to the Prophet and he was reciting: 'The mutual rivalry (for piling up worldly things) diverts you.' He said: 'The son of Adam says: 'My wealth, my wealth.' And do you own anything except what you eat such that you've finished it, or what you wear, such that you've worn it out, or what you give in charity, such that you've spent it? ***Khalid ibn Umair reported:*** I heard Utba b. Ghazwan as saying: I found myself as the seventh amongst the seven who had been along with Allah's Messenger (ﷺ). We had nothing to eat but the leaves of hubla (a wild tree) until the corners of our mouths were injured. **Narrated Sa`d:** I was the first man among the Arabs to throw an arrow for Allah's Cause. We used to fight in Allah's Cause while we had nothing to eat except the leaves of the Hubla and the Sumur trees (desert trees) so that we discharged excrement like that of sheep (i.e. unmixed droppings). *Amer narrated:* The Messenger of Allah, Abo Bakr, and Omar ate meat, barely bread, ripe dates, and cold water and said: 'By Allah, this is indeed the bounty'. *Abo Salama was heard narrating:* The Messenger of Allah (ﷺ) went out with one of his friends to Abo Al-Haytham ibn Tayhan- he is Malik ibn Tayhan- and entered to his wife and said: 'where is Abo Al-haytham?'. She said: 'He has gone to fetch us some good water'. Then, he came and told his wife: 'Woe to you! Did not you make something for the Messenger of Allah (ﷺ)?'. She said: 'No'. He said: 'get up'. She brought barely and have ground it and he brought a sheep and slaughtered female one. The Messenger of Allah (ﷺ) said: 'don't slaughter those that are lactating'. He cooked for them and presented to their hands, then they ate, then they drank bucket of water along with people'. The Messenger of Allah (ﷺ) said: 'you will be asked about this drink'. Abo Ka'b narrated: The Messenger of Allah (ﷺ) said: 'preach this nation with serenity, victory and empowerment. He who did the work of the Hereafter to the benefit of this world had no share in the Hereafter'. **Abo Ka'b narrated:** 'who made his biggest concern other than Allah, the Mighty and Sublime, he will not be from those who belong to Allah'. **Soliman ibn Habib said:** The Prophet (ﷺ) said: 'Whoever focuses all his concerns on one thing, the Hereafter, Allah will relieve him of his concerns, but whoever has disparate concerns scattered among a number of worldly issues, Allah will not care by which he dies'. **Al Hassan narrated:** 'Whoever makes the Hereafter his goal, Allah protects him against loss and makes his heart rich. And whoever makes the world his goal, Allah brings him to losses and puts his poverty right before his eyes, he will sleep and wake up in poverty'. **Abdur-Rahman ibn Aban ibn 'Uthman ibn 'Affan narrated that his father said:** 'Zaid ibn Thabit departed from Marwan at mid-day. I said: 'He has not sent him out at this time of the day except for something he asked.' So I asked him, and he said: 'He asked me about some things we heard from the Messenger of Allah (ﷺ) .I heard the Messenger of Allah (ﷺ) "May Allah cause to flourish a slave (of His) who hears my words and understands them, then he conveys them from me. There are

Asceticism - Part 1 -

those who have knowledge but no understanding, and there may be those who convey knowledge to those who may have more understanding of it than they do. There are three with which the heart of a Muslim shall not be deceived. Sincerity in deeds for Allah, giving advices to the A'immah of Muslims, and sticking to the Jama'ah. For indeed the call is protected from behind them. Whoever is focused on the Hereafter, Allah will settle his affairs for him and make him feel content with his lost, and his provision and worldly gains will undoubtedly come to him.' whoever makes the world his goal, Allah puts his poverty right before his eyes, and disorganizes his affairs, and the world does not come to him, except what has been decreed for him.' We asked him about the middle prayer which is the prayer of dhuhr.

Ibn Abbas (May Allah be pleased with him) reported:

Messenger of Allah (ﷺ) said, 'There are two blessings in which many people incur loss. (They are) free time (for doing good) and health'. *Abdullah ibn Busr narrated that two Bedouins said:* 'O Messenger of Allah! Who is the best of the people?' He said: 'He whose life is long and his deeds are good.' Other said: 'O Messenger of Allah. There are many injunctions of Islam for me. So, tell me something to which I may hold fast.' He said, 'Keep your tongue wet with the remembrance of Allah'. **Narrated Jubair ibn Nufair:** the Prophet (ﷺ) said: 'You shall not return to Allah with what is more virtuous than what came from Him.' Meaning the Qur'an.

Abu Hurairah narrated that the Messenger of Allah (ﷺ) said: 'Indeed Allah, Most High said: 'O son of Adam! Devote yourself to My worship, I will fill your chest with riches and alleviate your poverty. And if you do not do so, then I will fill your hands with problems and not alleviate your poverty'.

Fadalah ibn 'Ubaid (May Allah be pleased with him) reported: When the Messenger of Allah (ﷺ) led Salat, some people would fall down from their standing posture out of extreme hunger. They were of the people of As-Suffah. The nomad Arabs would say that they were insane. After concluding Salat, Messenger of Allah (ﷺ) would turn to them and say, 'If you were to know what is in store for you with Allah, the Exalted, you would wish to augment your starvation and lack of provisions.' Fadalah said:' I am with the Messenger of Allah (ﷺ) that day'. ***Al-Alaa ibn Bashir Al Mazny reported:*** the Messenger of Allah (ﷺ): I never witnessed such a brave when meeting God, crying when mentioning God'. ***Narrated Abu Sa'id al-Khudri:*** I was sitting in the company of Ansar. Some of us were sitting together because of lack of clothing while a reader was reciting to us Book of Allah, the Mighty and Sublime, All of a sudden the Messenger of Allah (ﷺ) came along and stood beside us. When the Messenger of Allah (ﷺ) stood, the reader stopped. He asked: What were you saying? We said: Messenger of Allah! We had a reader who was reciting to us and we were listening to the Book of Allah, the Exalted. The Messenger of Allah (ﷺ) had made a sign with his hand they sat in a circle. The narrator said: I think that the Messenger of Allah (ﷺ) did not recognize any of them except me. The Messenger of Allah (ﷺ) then said: Rejoice, you group of poor emigrants, in the announcement that you will have perfect light on the Day of Resurrection. You will enter Paradise half a day before the rich, and that is five hundred years.

Abu Hurairah (may Allah be pleased with him) narrated that the Messenger of Allah (ﷺ) said: 'If people sit in an assembly in which they do not remember Allah or invoke blessings on the Prophet it will be a cause of grief to them on the Day of Resurrection, even if they go to Paradise for reward'. ***It was narrated that Anas said:*** 'The Messenger of Allah had a she-camel called Al-'Adba' which could not be beaten. One day a Bedouin came on a riding-camel and beat her (in a race). The Muslims were upset by that, and when he saw the expressions on their faces they said: 'O Messenger of Allah, Al-'Adba' has been beaten.' He said: 'It is a right upon Allah that nothing is raised in this world except He lowers it'. ***Shaddad ibn Aus (May Allah be pleased with him) reported:*** The Prophet (ﷺ) said, 'A wise man is the one who calls himself to account (and refrains from doing evil deeds) and does noble deeds to benefit him after death; and the foolish person is the one who subdues himself to his temptations and desires and seeks from Allah'. While the Messenger of Allah (ﷺ) was talking to his companions when a poor man came and sat next to a man from the rich, as if he had seized his clothes. So, the Messenger of Allah (ﷺ) changed and said, "Oh, are you afraid that your richness turns to him and his poverty turns to you? He said, O Messenger of Allah, is richness is evil thing? He said: yes that your richness invites you to Hell and that his poverty invites him to Paradise'. He said, "What will save me?" He said: console him. He said, then I do this. The other said: and the other said :I don't seek it. He said: then seek forgiveness from God and pray to your brother. ***Abu Sa'id Al-Khudri (May Allah be pleased with him) reported:*** The Messenger of Allah (ﷺ) said: 'The world is sweet and green .So, beware of this world and beware of women' .***Mu`adh ibn Anas Al-Gahny (May Allah be pleased with him) reported:*** The Messenger of Allah (ﷺ) said, 'Whoever gives up wearing elegant and expensive garments out of humbleness, when he can do so, Allah will call him on the Day of Resurrection and before all the creations, He will give him the choice to wear whichever garment of Iman he would like to wear'. ***Anas ibn Malik narrated:*** Fatima (May Allah be pleased with her) handed piece of barely bread to the Messenger of Allah (ﷺ) then said: this is the first food your father shall eat since three days'. *It was narrated from 'Aishah that:* The Prophet (ﷺ) used to say: O Allah, make me one of those who, if they do good deeds, they rejoice, and if they do bad deeds, they seek forgiveness'. ***Al-Agharr - a man from Juhayna- reported*** that Ibn 'Umar stated to him that Allah's Messenger (ﷺ) said: 'O people, seek repentance from Allah. Verily, I seek repentance from Him a hundred times a day'. ***Jundub reported*** Allah's Messenger (ﷺ) as saying: He who wants to publicize (his deeds), Allah will publicize (his humility), and he who makes a hypocritical display (of his deeds), Allah will make a display of him. *It was narrated from Abu Hurairah that the Messenger of Allah (ﷺ) said:* 'There are people who fast and get nothing from their fast except hunger, and there are those who pray and get nothing from their prayer but a sleepless night'. ***Abu Hurairah (May Allah be pleased with him) reported:*** The Prophet (ﷺ) said, 'If one does not eschew lies and false conduct, Allah has no need that he should abstain from his food and his drink'. ***Abu Hurairah (May Allah be pleased with him) said:*** The Messenger of Allah (ﷺ) said, 'Almighty Allah says, 'I am the One Who is the best partner. He who does a thing for the sake of someone else beside Me, I shall be free from him'. Anas ibn Malik narrated: Allah's Messenger (ﷺ) said: one night I passed on people whose lips were being cut by the knife of fire, so I asked: who are they? He said: They are the speakers of your Ummah who used to enjoin virtue upon people but refrained to implement it on themselves and they studied the book (of Allah) (so) didn't they have any sense?. ***Abo Thor narrated:*** The Messenger of Allah (ﷺ) recited this verse: ' 'And whosoever fears Allah, He will make a way out for him.' Until he finished this verse then said' O Abo Thor, if all people follow this verse, it shall protect them'. He said:' He kept reciting and repeating it to me until I fell asleep'. **Ibn Umar narrated that:** The Messenger of Allah said: 'Whoever wishes to look at the Day of Resurrection, as if he is seeing it with this eye, then let him recite: 'When the sun Kuwwirat'. ***Ibn 'Abbas narrated that:*** the Messenger of Allah (ﷺ) turned to someone and said: By Whom Mohamed soul is in His Hands, I feel unhappy when someone transfers to the family of Muhamed gold which he spent in the way of Allah. When I die I left two dinars except those two dinars which he arranged for his faith. He said: he dies and left neither a dinar nor a dirham nor a male slave nor a female slave, and his armor was pawned to a Jew for thirty Sa's of barley'. Sa'eed ibn yazid narrated: a man heard The Prophet (ﷺ) saying: I advise you to be ashamed from God same as you feel ashamed from a good man in your nation'.

Hufs ibn Asem narrated: The Prophet (ﷺ) said, 'It is enough for a man to prove himself a liar. *Ghandar said*: It's a sin to tell everything he hears.' **Abo Saleh narrated** that one of the friends of The Messenger of Allah said: 'O Messenger of Allah, advise me of a deed that leads me to Heaven 'The Messenger of Allah (ﷺ) said: 'Do not get angry'. *Anas narrated:* The Messenger of Allah said:' The slave is fine as long as he is not impatient'. It was said: 'How he becomes impatient?'. He said: That he should say like this: I supplicated, and I supplicated but I did not find it being responded'.*Ma'qil ibn Yasar (May Allah be pleased with him) reported:* The Messenger of Allah (ﷺ) said 'The reward of worship performed at a time of trials is equal in reward to an emigration to me'. *Abu Huraira reported Allah's Messenger (ﷺ) as saying:* Verily Allah does not look to your faces and your wealth, but He looks to your heart and to your deeds. *Omar ibn Khattab narrated:* I heard The Messenger of Allah (ﷺ) saying: ' Who cares about people got humiliated by God'. ***Abdullah ibn Mas'od narrated:*** The Messenger of Allah (ﷺ) said 'Then on that Day, you shall be asked about the delights!' He said: Safety and health'. ***Abo Muslim Al-Kholany*** heard The Messenger of Allah (ﷺ) saying: ' God did not advised me to collect money and be a merchant, rather he advised me to celebrate the glory of God and be one of the prostrators'. ***Obid ibn Omir narrated:*** The Messenger of Allah (ﷺ) said: 'You find the believer strives in what he is capable of doing, and curious to do what is not capable of doing'. ***Ibn Saleh A-Hafny narrated:***

The Messenger of Allah (ﷺ) said: 'God is merciful, and does not apply his mercy except on the merciful, and does not grant Heaven except for the merciful' .They said: O The Messenger of Allah, we mercy our money and our family'. He said:' That's not it, rather what God said: 'He is eager for you; for the believers (he is) full of pity, kind, and merciful'. ***Bakr ibn Sawadah narrated:*** The Messenger of Allah (ﷺ) said : There will be amongst my nation those who are born in bliss and feed from it, they care about the colors of food and cloth, who are diffuse in speech, those are the worst of my nation'.

Asceticism - Part 1 -

Al Hassan narrated: The Messenger of Allah (ﷺ) said: The believer is who is entrusted by people, the emigrant is who abandoned the evil, Muslim whom his neighbor feels safe towards him, By Him in Whose Hand my soul is! He will not enter Jannah whose neighbour is not secure from his wrongful conduct'. **Abu Hurairah narrated that the Messenger of Allah (ﷺ) said:** 'Indeed a man may utter a statement which he does not see any harm in, but for which he will fall seventy autumns in the Fire'. *'Aisha (God's mercy be upon her) narrated :* The Messenger of Allah (ﷺ) worked in his home and what he worked the most is sewing'. Al Hassan narrated: The Messenger of Allah(ﷺ) would not close the doors in the face of his people, and he was so humble, he was a prominent person. Who wants to meet the Prophet of God he will meet him? He was sitting on the ground and his food was placed on the ground and he was wearing the heavy clothes and riding the donkey. He responds to people and licks his hand. *Hakim ibn Omir narrated:* The Messenger of Allah (ﷺ) said: 'He to whom the blessing door has been opened, he must take advantage of it, he does not know when this door shall be closed'. *Hoshab narrated:* The Messenger of Allah (ﷺ) said:

Oh God, I seek refuge in you from the world that prevents the good of work and seek refuge in you from the world that prevents the good of death'. ***Al Hassan narrated:*** The Messenger of Allah (ﷺ) said: when a group of people sit remembering God, the Mighty and Sublime, God says to His angels I forgave them, overwhelm them with mercy. Angels say: O God, so and so is one of them. He says: they are who are sitting together, and the one who sits with them does not afflict them. ***Al Hagag ibn Al-Aswad narrated:*** Al-Hassan and Hussein were hungry, and they were sent to nine houses from the houses of the Messenger of Allah (ﷺ). They did not find neither wet nor dry food to eat'. ***'Aisha (Mercy be upon her) said:*** ' By Who sent Mohammed with truth, he (Messenger of Allah (ﷺ) never saw a sieve, and never ate ground bread, since he was born till he died'. It was said: "How were you eating barely?" She said: "we were saying Off Off'. ***Al Hassan narrated:*** The Prophet (ﷺ) said, 'The son of Adam is questioned about everything except about these three things: A cloth to cover therewith his private parts, food to build his body, a house to live in. What comes above that, he is questioned about'. ***Al Hassan narrated:*** 'The Messenger of Allah said:' The slave performs a sin and enter by his sin to Paradise: He said: O Messenger of God; how he enters Paradise? He said,

Asceticism - Part 1 -

'The sin is still in front of his sight, and he is fleeing from it until he enters Paradise'. **Sa'eed ibn Al Moseeb narrated:** The Messenger of Allah (peace and blessings of Allah be upon him) when hears the voice of the sky (Thunder) this always is seen in his face, until it rains, he feels comfort. It was said to him: What is this that we see in your face, O Messenger of Allaah? He said: 'I do not know I ordered mercy or punishment'.

Omar ibn Khattab narrated: 'I entered upon the Prophet (ﷺ) when he was suffering from a fever, I placed my hand on his garment and felt heat above the garment. I said: 'O Messenger of Allah, how hard it is for you!' He said: 'This is how God multiplied reward for us. The Prophets are the most severely tested, then the righteous, some of whom were tested with poverty until they could not find anything except a cloak to put around themselves. Some of them are overcome by lice until they kill them'. **Mohamed Ibn Motraf narrated:** That a boy from Ansar entered his heart fear of Hell, that he stayed in the house. The Messenger of Allah (ﷺ) came to his house, hugged him then the man sobbed and died. The Messenger of Allah (ﷺ): 'Prepare your friend, the fear from Hell killed him'. *It was narrated that Abu Hurairah said:* 'The Prophet said: What most leads a man to Hell are the two hollow things: the mouth and the private part, and what most admits people to

Paradise are piety and good manners.' ***Asad ibn Dera'a narrated:*** 'The Messenger of Allah was asked: 'Which of the believers is the best?'. He said: 'Whose heart is pure and sincere, with no rancor or envy in it. They said:' O Messenger of Allah, this is not amongst us.' They said:' Which of the next believers is the best?'. He said: 'who is lessening life, seeking the hereafter. They said:' O Messenger of Allah, this is not amongst us.' Rafe' ibn Khadeej said:' Which of the next believers is the best?'. He said:' who is with good manners'.

Abu Huraira reported Allah's Messenger (ﷺ) as saying:

There is none whose deeds alone can secure salvation for him. They said: Allah's Messenger (ﷺ), not even you? Thereupon he said: Not even me, but that, the Mercy of Allah should take hold of me, and worship Allah in the forenoon and in the afternoon and during a part of the night, and always adopt a middle, moderate, regular course whereby you will reach your target (Paradise). **'Anas narrated that the Messenger of Allah (ﷺ) said:**

'When Allah wants good for a slave, He puts him in action.' It was said: 'How does he put him in action O Messenger of Allah?' He said: 'By making him meet up with the righteous deeds before death'. ***Al Hassan narrated:*** one of the best friends of the Messenger of Allah degraded a man by his mother, the

Messenger of Allah (ﷺ) heard and said: By Allah, you are not better than what you see here from red and black, except by only piety'. ***Al Hassan narrated:*** the Messenger of Allah (ﷺ) said:' By Allah, life does not worth to Allah, the mighty and sublime, a goat from the sheep'. **Abu Hurairah (May Allah be pleased with him) reported:** The Prophet (ﷺ) said, 'Richness is not the abundance of wealth, rather it is self-sufficiency'. ***Shaddad ibn Aws's sister narrated*** that she sent to The Prophet (ﷺ) upon breakfast during the day when it was very hot. The Prophet (ﷺ) said: from where you got this milk?'. She said: 'from one of my goats'. The Prophet (ﷺ) said: 'from where you got this goat?'. She said: 'I bought it from my money'. Then he drank it. The following day, Om Abdullah came to the Prophet (ﷺ) and said: 'O Messenger of Allah, I sent you this milk twice due to long day and hot weather, but you sent it back to me. The Messenger of Allah (ﷺ) said: I ordered the messengers before me not to eat except the good, and not to act except the good deeds'. ***Al Hassan said:*** The Prophet (ﷺ) was asked: which is the best deed? He said:' when you die while your tongue is kept wet with the remembrance of Allah, the Mighty and Sublime'. ***Atta' ibn***

Yassar narrated: The Prophet (ﷺ) said:' Life came to me green and beautiful, and decorated for me. I said to her I don't want you. No one escaped from me except you'. ***Anas ibn Malik said,*** 'I came to the Prophet, may Allah bless him and grant him peace, while he was on a seat with a bad woven on it. He had a pillow under his head made of skin stuffed with fibre. There was a cloth between his skin and the seat. 'Umar visited him and wept. The Prophet, may Allah bless him and grant him peace, said, 'What made you weep, 'Umar?' He said, 'By Allah, Messenger of Allah, I am only weeping since I know that you are more noble with Allah than Chosroes and Caesar. They both live in what they live of this world while you, Messenger of Allah, are in the place I see.' The Prophet, may Allah bless him and grant him peace, said, 'Are you not content, 'Umar, that they have this world while we have the Next?' I replied, 'Yes, Messenger of Allah.' He said, 'That is the way of it'. ***Nu'man b. Bashir reported:*** The Messenger of Allah (ﷺ) said: Verily the least suffering for the inhabitants of Fire would be for him who would have two shoes and two laces of Fire (on his feet), and with these would boil his brain as boils the cooking vessel, and he would think that he would not see anyone in a more grievous torment than him, whereas he would be in the least torment'. **'Aishah** (May Allah be pleased with her) narrated: The

Messenger of Allah (ﷺ) said: 'Do you know who is the first to reach God's shadow?'. They said: 'Allah and His Prophet know better. He said:' Those who accept the truth when given to them, and who give truth when they are asked about it, and who judge between people as they judge on themselves'. **Othman Al Nahdy narrated:** The Messenger of Allah (ﷺ) said: 'The people of correctness in this world are the people of correctness in the Next World. The people of the incorrect in this world are the people of the incorrect in the Hereafter'. **Wahb ibn Munabbih narrated:** The Messenger of Allah (ﷺ) said: 'When Allah loves people, He tests them'. **Mus'ab ibn Sa'd narrated from his father:** I said'

'O Messenger of Allah which of the people is tested most severely?' He said: 'The Prophets, then the righteous, then those nearest to them, then those nearest to them. A person is tested according to his religious commitment. If he is steadfast in his religious commitment, he will be tested more severely, and if he is frail in his religious commitment, his test will be according to his commitment. Trials will continue to afflict a person until they leave him walking on the earth with no sin on him'. **Anas ibn Malik narrated:** 'Why haven't I seen Mikhail laughing ever?'. He said: 'Mikhail

Never laughed since fire has been created'. ***Malik ibn Abi Al Gawzaa narrated:*** The Messenger of Allah (ﷺ) said: 'increase the remembrance of God until the hypocrites think you are hypocrites'. ***Al Hassan narrated:*** The Messenger of Allah (ﷺ) said: 'God does not torture his beloved slave but may test him in life'. ***Fatima ibn Hussein narrated:*** The Messenger of Allah (ﷺ) said: 'The worst of my community are those who had lots of blessings, those who request variety of food and cloths, those who are diffuse in speech'.

Mohamed ibn Sairen narrated: that the Messenger of Allah (ﷺ) entered to Bilal (God's mercy be upon him) when he saw a bowl of dates in his house, then he said: ' what is this?'. He said: 'this is dates which I saved'. He said: 'you are afraid that it shall has smoke in the Fire of Hell. O Bilal spend whatever you wish, and do not fear any lessening from the Lord of the 'Arsh (Throne)'.

Abo A Melih ibn Ma'mon narrated: 'The Prophet (ﷺ) has nothing from life virtues except women and fragrance'.

• CHAPTER 2 •

Adam asceticism (Peace be upon him)

Salman (May Allah be pleased with him) narrated: when God, the Mighty and Sublime, created Adam (Peace be upon him) He said: One for Me, one for you, one between Me and you , What is Mine, you worship Me and do not worship others besides Me. As for what is yours, I reward you for what you did for Me. I forgive as I am Forgiving and Merciful. As for what is between Me and you, that's du'aa 'and I have to answer and grant'. ***Bakr narrated:*** when Adam was offered his offspring, he saw each other's favor on one another. He said : 'O Lord, have you treated them equally? He said: 'O Adam, I loved to be thanked'. ***Ibrahem said:*** Thanking him is to say ''Bismillah' before we began eating, and thank him after he finishes. ***Alqama***

ibn Marthad narrated: If all the people on earth cried, their tears would not be equal to that of Dawud (peace be upon him) when he sinned, and the tears of the people on earth and the tears of Dawud (peace be upon him) would not be equal to that of Adam when he put down on earth'. ***Al Hassan narrated:*** Adam (peace be upon him) stayed one hour I heaven, this hour equals to a hundred and thirty days from life days. ***Mo'bad Al Gahny narrated:*** what forced Adam (peace be upon him) to eat the tree is poverty. ***Sa'eed ibn Jabeer narrated:*** Adam (peace be upon him) stayed in Heaven only between noon and afternoon. ***Al Hassan narrated:*** before Adam (peace be upon him) committed a sin, he put his death in front of his eyes and his hope behind his back. When he commits it, he put his death in front of his eyes and his hope behind his back. ***Shoin Al Geba'y narrated:*** the tree which God, the Mighty and Sublime, when forbid Adam and his wife from eating was called 'Al Da'aa' and their cloths were light'. ***Anas ibn Mlik narrated:*** when God, the Mighty and Sublime, created Adam (peace be upon him), he made Devil go around him looking at him. When he saw him impatient, he knew he can be seduced. ***Abo Ka'b narrated:*** The Messenger of Allah (ﷺ) said: Adam was a tall like a palm tree, his head was full of hair, when he fell his private part appeared to him- he did not see it before then- then he ran away with a tree from Paradise's trees. He said to it: send me, it said: I am not your sender. He said that God, the Mighty and Sublime, called him: O Adam do you ran away from me? He said: Lord, no, but I am ashamed from you'. He said: He called him saying: the believer gets ashamed from God if he commits a sin, then he knows, than with thanking God, he will get away from it'. ***Ibn Abbas narrated:*** when religion verse came down, The Messenger of Allah (ﷺ) said: When God created and wiped his back, He took out my descendants to the Day of Resurrection, and He showed his descendants to him, and he saw a blossom man'. He said: O Lord, who is this? He said: This is your son Dawud. He said: O Lord, how old is he? He said: Sixty years. He said: "O Lord, add to his age." He said, "No, but I will increase him from your age. Adam was a thousand years old, and he added him forty years old. So, God wrote a book on that and let the angels witness that'. When Adam died, the angels came to him to take his soul. and said: I still have forty years. He was told: You have given it to your son Dawud. He said: I have not. God, the Mighty and Sublime, showed him the book and the angels witnessed, then He completed a hundred years to Dawud, and Adam a thousand years".

• CHAPTER 3 •

Noah asceticism (Peace be upon him)

Waheeb ibn Al Ward narrated: When Allah, the Mighty and Sublime asked Noah about his son, he said the verse: 'I admonish you, lest you should be among the ignorant.''

Obeid ibn Omair narrated: The people of Noah attacked him to the point that he fainted and when getting up, he said: O Allah! Forgive my people, because they certainly do not know'. Obeid ibn Omair narrated: a man from Noah people strangled him to the point that he fainted and when getting up, he said: O Allah! Forgive my people, because they certainly do not know'. Mohamed ibn Ka'b Al Karthy narrated: When Noah was eating food, or drinking water, or wearing clothes, or riding he thanked God.　God called him' a grateful servant'. Atta ibn Yasar narrated: The Messenger of Allah (ﷺ) said: the Prophet Nouh, may Allah bless him and grant him peace, told his son, 'I will give you some instructions. I command you two things and I forbid you two things. The two things I command you are those which requested by God so much and He rejoices with the most for all his creatures. I command you to say, ' Sobhan Allah wabehamdeh'.. ' It is the prayer of everything and by it everything has its provision. Also, to say 'There is no God but Allah. ' If the seven heavens and the seven earths were a dark ring, they would be cut by. As for the two things I forbid you are disbelief in Me and arrogance. If you can meet Allah, the Mighty and Sublime with no disbelief or arrogance in your heart, then do it'.

Abdullah ibn Omar said: The Messenger of Allah (ﷺ) said: Noah, peace be upon him, advised his son (he referred to the above-mentioned Hadith) saying: 'As for the two things I forbid you are disbelief in Me and arrogance. Abdullah ibn Omar said: O Messenger of Allah, is arrogance to have beautiful accessories to wear?'. He said: No! God is beautiful and He loves beauty'. He said: 'Is arrogance to have an animal to ride?'. He said: 'No'. He said: 'Is arrogance to have friends following me and I feed them?'. He said: 'No'. He said: 'then, what is arrogance Messenger of Allah?'. He said: 'to depreciate truth and disgrace it'. Ali said:' I said to Hesham: how to disgrace? He said:' discredit it'. Mosa ibn Ali ibn Rabbah narrated that his father

Asceticism - Part 1 -

heard Noah, may Allah bless him and grant him peace, saying to his son:' O son, do not enter crave with an ant's weight of arrogance in your heart. Arrogance is the cloth of Allah, the Mighty and Sublime, who compete God in his cloth, makes Him angry. 'O son do not enter crave with an ant's weight of despair. No one is desperate from God's mercy except the distorted'. Al Hassan narrated that Noah, may Allah bless him and grant him peace, did not call against his people until this verse' And it was inspired in Noah, (saying): No-one of thy folk will believe save him who hath believed already. Be not distressed because of what they do'. Then, his hope has cut from them, and he called against them.

CHAPTER 4

Ibrahem Al-Khalil asceticism (Peace be upon him)

Ka'b narrated : Ibrahem (peace be upon him) said: O Lord, I am saddened that I see no one in the earth worship you except me, God, the Mighty and Sublime, sent angels to pray with him and be with him'. Ka'b in his saying: 'Verily, Ibrahim was, without doubt, forbearing, used to invoke Allah with humility, and was repentant'. He said: 'when he mentions Hell, he said O how I fear the hot fire!. ***Ibn Abi Malika narrated:*** when Ibrahim, peace be upon him, died, God, Almighty and Sublime, said to him, 'Ibrahem, how did you find death? He said: O Lord, I found myself suffering from scourge. It was said:' we made it easy for you'. ***Abo Othman narrated:*** two lions were sent to

Ibrahem, they were hungry. They licked him and prostrated to him'. Ali, peace be upon him, narrated: 'O Fire! be thou cool, and (a means of) safety for Abraham!'. If he did not say 'safety', he would have been killed by its cold'. *Al Hareth ibn Ali, peace be upon him, narrated:* The first one to be clothed on the Day of Resurrection will be Ibrahim with cotton cloth, then The Prophet (ﷺ) clothed by petechia cloth while he is on the right side of the Throne'. Abdel Malik ibn Noof Al-Bekali narrated: Ibrahem (peace be upon him) said: O Lord, there is no one on earth worshiping except me. He said: Allah has revealed three thousand kings, and he led them for three days. *Bakr narrated:* when Ibrahim (peace be upon him) was thrown in fire, all people from the public claimed to their lord, and said: O Lord, your mate is thrown into the fire, let us extinguish it for him. He said: He is my mate, there is no other mates in the land, He said, He has no God but me. If he seeks refuge from you, then do it or let him. Then, Qatar king came and said: O Lord, your mate is thrown into the fire, let me extinguish it for him. He said, He has no God but me. If he seeks refuge from you, then do it or let him. When he was thrown into the fire, he prayed for God, God, the Mighty and Sublime said, O fire! Be you cool and safety for Ibrahim! Then it was extinguished on all people from East and west and did not produce anything". *Sa'eed ibn Jaber narrated:* when Ibrahim (peace be upon him) saw Ishak slaughter in his dream, he walked with him from his home to the slaughtering place, a month walk done in one day. When the slaughter was put away from him and was ordered to slaughter the sheep, then went back to his house, for one month walk in one night. Mountains and valleys were made easy to him. *It was narrated from Sa'ibah,* the freed slave woman of Fakih ibn Mughirah, that she entered upon 'Aishah and saw a spear in her house. She said: "O Mother of the Believers, what do you do with this?" She said: "We kill these house lizards with it, for the Prophet of Allah (ﷺ) told us that when Ibrahim was thrown into the fire, there was no beast on earth that did not try to put it out, apart from the house lizard that blew on it. So, the Messenger of Allah (ﷺ) commanded that they should be killed.'. *Anas ibn Malik narrated that:* A man said to the Prophet: "O best of creatures!" So, he said: "That is Ibrahim."

• CHAPTER 5 •

Joseph asceticism (Peace be upon him)

Yahya ibn Selim narrated: Jacob, the most generous on earth, said: The angel of death, peace be upon him, asked God's permission to come to Jacob, then he permitted him. He came to him, then Jacob told him: O angel of death, by who created you, have you captured Joseph's soul among those souls you captured? He said no. The angel of death said: O Jacob, shall I teach you words? He said: yes. He said: Say: O who owns favor which You only can count. He said: Jacob invoked that night, that the dawn did not came out until the shirt was put on his face then he had the sight'. ***Abdulah Mo'then Al-Ta'ef narrated:*** Jibril came to Yousef (ﷺ) and said: O Yousef, prison became hard on you? He said: Yes. He said: say (O Allah, relieve me from all my misery and sadness in my life and my hereafter and lead me to the way out, and provide me from (sources) I never can imagine, forgive me my sin, and set my hope and cut it off from others, so that I will not seek anyone else". ***Al Hassan narrated:*** The Messenger of Allah (ﷺ): May Allah have mercy on Yousef, if I had not spoken to him, he would not stay in prison as long as he stayed, his saying: Mention me in the presence of thy lord. Al Hassan cried and said: when we face an issue, we rush to people. ***Al Hassan narrated:*** The Messenger of Allah (ﷺ): May Allah have mercy on Yousef, if the messenger came to me after stayed long time in prison, I would respond quickly'. ***Al Hassan narrated:*** Yousef was put in prison when he was seventeen years old, he was in slavery and prison and kingdom for eighty years, then he re-joined with his family and lived fifty-three years'. ***Anas narrated:*** God, the Mighty and Sublime, inspired Joseph: Who survived you from murder, are they your brothers? He said, "It's You, O Lord" He said:" then, why you mention a human and forgot Me? " He said: He said: O Lord, it's just a word spoken by my tongue". He said: By My Glory, I will put you in prison for years". ***Al Hassan narrated:*** "Jacob cried on Joseph for eighty year, and he was then the most generous upon earth to Allah, the Mighty and Sublime'. ***Al Hassan narrated:*** there was eighty years between the dream (Joseph's dream) and the interpretation'. ***Habib***

Asceticism - Part 1 -

narrated: a man passed by Jacob while his eyebrows fell down on his eyes, he lifted them with a band, he said: O God's Prophet, what led you to this condition? He said: The length of time and the abundance of grief. Then, God inspired to Him: O Jacob, do you complain from me? He said: O God, it's a sin, please forgive me'.

• CHAPTER 6 •

Ayyub-Job- asceticism (Peace be upon him)

Al Hassan narrated: There were nothing left from Ayyub except his eyes, heart, and tongue, the animals got confused about his body. He said: Prophet Ayyub had been left on the pile of garbage of Bani Israel for seven years and days or (he said) months. **Abdullah ibn Omeir** narrated: Ayyub (peace be upon him) had two brothers who came to him one day and they found a wind, and they said: If God knew good from Ayyub, nothing from all what happened would happen to him'. He said: He would not hear something more severe than that, he said: "Oh God, if you know that I did not sleep a night while I know the place of a hungry man then believe me. He said: He believed him while they hear'. He said: Oh God, if you know that I did not wear a shirt while I know the place of naked man then believe me. He said: He believed him while they hear'. Then he prostrated, and said, "O God, I will not lift my head until you reveal what I have'. Then God, the Mighty and Sublime, revealed what he has'. Then he emphasizes on the same Sanad and says: If God knew good from Ayyub, nothing from all what happened would happen to him'. ***Aqil narrated*** he had heard Ibn Monabeh was asked: what was the legislation of Ayyub - peace be upon him - he said: "Tawheed and Salah between them, and if one wanted to seek help from God, Almighty and Sublime, he shall prostrate then ask for his help'. It was said: how much money he owned?' He said: He had three thousand acres, a slave with each acre, and with every slave a child, and with each child of female donkey and fourteen thousand sheep, and no guest remained behind his door, and he never ate food except with a poor man'. ***Wahb was heard saying:*** Ayoub suffered affliction for seven years'. ***Noof Al-Bakai narrated:*** one of Bani Israel passed by Ayyub - peace be upon him - and said: What had happened to him was due to a great sin he committed. Ayyub heard that then said: "Lord, I was touched by the evil and you are the Most-Merciful of those who have mercy'. He said: He was not invoking before then'. ***Ibn Oyayna narrated:*** When all this bad happened to Ayyub, peace be upon him, he sent to his companions, and he said: Do you know why this happened to me? They said: for us, we did not see anything you did, except if you have done something that we don't know. They left him and met someone lower than them in knowledge, he said: why did Prophet of God called you? They told him then he said: I tell you what happened to him. He brought him and asked him, he said: 'Because you drank a drink and did not thank God for it, and you did not thank the blessing, and you were shaded in a shadow and did not thank the blessing". Bakr narrated: When Allah forgave Ayyub (peace be upon him), he rained at him a jar of gold upon him. He said: He kept collecting. He said: God called him: 'O Ayyub, Haven't I made you rich? Are you not satisfied? He said: O Lord, and who satisfies from your blessing?'. ***Abdel Rahman ibn Jabir narrated:*** When the Prophet of God, Ayyub, was afflicted with his money, his son and his body, and he was put in a dustibn, his wife came out to earn to feed him. The devil envied him for that, that he went to the owners of bread and barbecues whom they were giving her charity and said to them: drive this woman out who is cheating you. They did not come close to her and said: stay away from us, we feed you and don't come close to us. So, she told Ayoub, he thanked God, Almighty and Sublime, for that and said to her: You have met the enemy of God and told you this speech. When God gave us money and child safe, we believed in Him, then when He takes what He Owns from us, we disbelieve in Him. If God raised me from this disease, I will lash you a hundred lashes. So, God, Almighty and Sublime, said "And take in thy hand a little grass, and strike therewith: and break not (thy oath). He means (a bunch). **Talha narrated:** Iblis said: "I have never got anything from Job which I am glad of, except that when I heard him wailing, I knew that I had hurt him'. **Al Mubarak ibn Fadala narrated:** Ayoub (peace be upon him) whenever he suffered a calamity said: Oh God, You tak and You give, however I will keep myself thanking You on the good tests You give me'. Dawood narrated: The Prophet (ﷺ) said: Ayoub was the most patient, the most kind, and the most who can block his anger'.

• CHAPTER 7 •

Younus – Jonah-asceticism (Peace be upon him)

Qatada said: God, Almighty and Sublime, said: Had he not been of them who glorify Allah'. He said: He has done many prayers in prosperity. He said: the good deed raises his companion if he stumbled, and if he knocks down, he will find a banquet'. **Salem ibn Abi Alja'd narrated:** God, Almighty and Sublime, said: 'he cried through the depths of darkness'. God inspired the whale not to scratch his meat nor break his bone, then another whale swallowed him then he cried in the darkness: the darkness of the whale, another whale and the sea'. Mojahed narrated: 'Seventy prophets pilgrimaged the house of Allah, including Moses the son of Imran, peace be upon him, wearing two cotton garments. He said: one of them was Younus, peace be upon him, saying: I am at Your service, who heal the grief'. ***Abo Al Galad narrated:*** The torment which fell upon the Yunus people, began to hover on their heads like the cuts of the dark night. The ones with minds went to Sheikh among the rest of their scientists, they said: it has come down to us what you see, so teach us a prayer that we invoke God, may God, Almighty and Sublime, to take out punishment from us. He said: they said: O Who is alive when no one is alive, Who is live not alive, and restore life to the dead, Who is live, no God but Allah. He said: then God, Almighty and Sublime, revealed about them'. ***Al Sha'by narrated*** about a man who said: Yunus stayed into the belly of the whale for forty days. Al Sha'by said: he stayed less than one day'. He swallowed at forenoon, then in the afternoon, and when the sun approached the sunset, the whale yawned, and he saw Yunus the light of the sun. "There is no god but thou: glory to thee: I was indeed wrong!". He said: And he threw him away and became like a chick'. A man told Al Saa'by: Do you deny the ability of God, Almighty and Sublime? He said: I do not deny the ability of God, Almighty and Sublime, if God, Almighty and Sublime, wanted to put market in its stomach he would do that. ***Abo Malik narrated:*** Yunus, peace be upon him, stayed in the whale's stomach for forty days.

• CHAPTER 8 •

Moses asceticism (Peace be upon him)

Wahb narrated that he heard Al-Khadr telling Moses when he met him: O Moses ibn Emran, stay away from stubbornness, and don't walk with no need, and don't laugh with no wonder. Stay at your home and cry for your sin'. Ibn Abbas narrated: when The Messenger of Allah (peace and blessings of Allah be upon him) sent Moses and Aaron to Pharaoh saying, "Do not be tempted by his cloths, because all his intention with my hand, and he does not utter nor close his eyes without my permission. And do not be tempted by the world flowers he enjoys and the adornment of those who are devout. If I would like to grant you the adornment of the world with something Pharaoh knows, his power is incapable of doing so, I would do that, and this is not because I don't care about you, however I grant you your share of dignity so that life does not deprive you from it. I protect my holy people from life same like the herder who is protecting his sheep from fetus. I also take them away like the herder who takes away his sheep from destruction places'. I want to enlighten their ranks and purify their hearts in them know characteristics and in which they are proud of it. I know that whoever fears another lord is competing me with enmity and I am the revolutionist to my holy people on the Day of Resurrection. **Wahb ibn Monbah narrated:** when Moses went near the fire, he noticed that the fire glittered from inside of a green branch and every moment it became brighter and more beautiful. He stood looking does not know what to do? He thought that it was a burning tree, one of its branches burned then the tree burned, but the fire was prevented by the intensity of its grass and multitude of water, and the density of its paper, and the hugeness of its trunk. He left it like that and stood up waiting for something to be dropped from it to take it. When it took time for this to happen, He bent to take some of it with the small piece of wood he had in his hand, but the fire came toward him. He terrified and came back. Sometimes he went toward the fire and sometimes the fire came towards him. Then, he returned and recirculate around it, as it still wants him, and he wants it. Nothing helps in its iniquity, then his wonder grew stronger. Moses thought about it, and said: It is a refraining fire, nothing can take out from it, but it is inflamed by a tree and does not burn it, and its iniquity is as much as its hugeness close to the twink of an eye'.

When Moses saw this, he said: "This fire is for a thing, and then he explained its condition that it was following an order or it's made so no one knows who ordered it, nor by which it was ordered, or who made it, or why it is made. He stood puzzled, did not know whether to return or stay? Then, he looked to its branch, which became greener than before. The green color is shining in the sky, he looked at it and fears darkness. The green is still shining, yellowing and whitening, until it became a bright light column between heaven and earth like the sunbeam by which the sights are dulled. Whenever he looked at him, he almost snatched his eyesight, and then his fear and grief intensified. He put his hand over his eyes and stuck to the ground. He heard the palpitations and the anguish, but then he heard something that the hearers have never heard of such intensity. When Moses reached the depths of distress, his horror became deep and his mind became almost confused due to the intensity of fear to hear and see. It was called out of the tree and was said: O Moses. He answered quickly and he did not know who called him. And the speed of his answer was only an appeal to humans

He said repeatedly: At your service, I hear your voice, I can hear you but cannot see you, where are you? He said: I am above you, with you and in front of you and closer to you than yourself. When Moses heard this, he learned that it should be only his God, Almighty, so he became ascertain of Him. He said: So you, O God, is this Your voice or Your messenger? God, Almighty said: This is Me who speaks to you so come close to Me. Moses gathered his hands in the stick, until he stood up, and his feet trembled, so that his legs were disordered, and his tongue was cut, and his heart were broken, there is nothing left of the bone carrying another. He became like the dead, but the spirit of life was running inside him. He kept crawling with horror until he stopped close to the tree that he was called from. God, Almighty, said: "And what is that in your right hand, O Moses?" He said, "It is my staff". He said:" What you use it for?"- no one knows better- Moses, peace be upon him, said: " I lean, and wherewith I beat down branches for my sheep and wherein I find other uses." Allah, Almighty, said, "Throw it down, O Moses." Moses thought that he said: reject it and threw it out of rejection, and then when he looked, he saw the greatest snake one can see, seeking and touching as if he wanted to take something, passing through the rock like a camel's foreman, picking it out, and tugging with his teeth at the root of the great tree then taking it out. His eyes were burning

Asceticism - Part 1 -

with fire. The stick had become like meteorites with fangs and teeth and had a sound. When Moses saw that, he ran away and did not return back. So, Moses went back to where he was, and he returned to see that he defeated the snake. He said, "Take it with your right hand." O Mouses, go back to it and lift it up again; We will make it exactly as it was before'. And Moses then wear a garment from wool with sticks, when he ordered him to take it, he bent the arm of the garment on his hand and said to him: see Moses, if Allah, Almighty, wishes he will do it, will the garment protect you? He said: "No, but I am weak and I have been created from weakness'. He revealed his hand and put it in the snake until it hears the sense of teeth and fangs. So, he found it returned to the stick he used to have and his hands were in the same place where he used to put when bending on the two sides of the stick. Allah, Almighty, told him: come closer'. As he was getting closer, he bent his back on the tree trunk, he rested, and his fear went away'. He gathered his hands in the stick and put down his head and neck and said: I have set you up today at a place that should not be held by any person after you. I let you come close to hear my words and you were in the closest places to me. Then deliver my message as you are now my ear and eye and you have my hand and victory. I have put on you heaven from my throne to add it to your power. You are a great soldier of my soldiers. I sent you to a weak people of my

AHMAD IBN HANBAL

creation, who ignored my grace and secured my cunning and seduced by life from me till he denied my right and denied my Lordship and worshiped other than Me and claimed he does not know me. I swear to my dignity if it wasn't for the excuse that was placed between me and my creatures, I would stack him severely that heavens, earth, mountains and seas would anger for his anger. If I ordered heaven it will ballast him, if I ordered earth, it would swallow him, If I ordered mountains they will destroy him, if I ordered seas, they would sink him, but I have no care about him anymore and he fell out of my eyes and my dream became large to him, and I dispensed with what I have, and this is my right as no one is richer than me. Then. Deliver my message to him and invite him to my worship and unification, and the sincerity of my name, and remind him of my days, and warn him of my indignation and curse, and tell him not to do what makes me angry, and tell between that an easy words so that he might remember or fear me, and inform him that I can pardon and forgive faster than getting angry and apply punishment, and do not be seduced with what I have dressed him from the dress of life, His forelock is in my hand, he cannot speak, utter, or breathe without my permission. Tell him: Answer your Lord; He is so forgiving, that he has give

Asceticism - Part 1 -

n   you four hundred years, and in all you are a swordsman to fight him, resemble and represent him, and get   his creatures away   from his path, and he   makes   the   sky raining on you, and the earth grant you grass. you did not repent, did not become   weak, did not get   poor, and did not   loose hope, and if he would wish to take all this from you, he would do that, but he is with a great dream. Fight on behalf of him with your brother, and you are calculated
for his jihad, if I want to bring him a huge number of soldiers, I would   do   that, but so   as to know this weak servant, who has admired   himself and his masses that the few   group can beat   the many only with my permission. don't like their decoration, nor the pleasures he has, and not look at that with your eyes; it is the flower of life, and decorations of the rich, if I wish to give you from the decorations of the world that when Pharaoh sees it, he will know that he is not capable of doing, I would do that. However, I take you away from this as this is what I do for my holy people. I chose this to them. I provide them with its delights and prosperity as Shepherd who is defending his camels from destruction places. I did not do that because of their insignificance to me but to complete their share of my dignity intact with large minimum range. Life did not hurt him nor take away his joy. I know that the best decorations that servants got

for me is the asceticism in life. It's the decoration of the pious who dress themselves with peacefulness and reverence. Their features are shown on their faces from prostration. Those are really my holy people. if you found them, put down your wing and humble your heart and tongue. Know that who insults my companion or feared him, he quarrels with me, and shows his soul and invited me to it. I am the fastest to uphold my companions. Does who quarrel me think he will overcome me? Does who fight me think he will defeat me? Does who fight me think he will precede or miss me? How can be that while I am the rebellious to them in this world and the Hereafter and do not move their support to others? He said: Moses, peace be upon him, came to Pharaoh in the city around which the lion her in the girdle had planted them, the lion with her politics if I paralyzed one ate it and the city four doors in the Ghaydah, MosesAllah be pleased with him came from the great road that Pharaoh can sees, and when the lion saw him, it starts to scream just as the foxes screaming, then the lords denied Pharaoh and get rid of him. After that, Moses came to the door where Pharaoh is and starts to knock it by his rod with a Jebba of wool and trousers on it. When the doorman saw him, he wondered from his courage, so, he left him and did not authorize him and said: Do you know whose door you are knocking? You knock the door of your Lord. He said: I, and you, and Pharaoh are servants of Allah Almighty, and I support him. So, he was told by the previous doorman, and he told the doorman that followed, and the next doormen until he reached the closest one, and in front of him seventy doormen, each one of them As Allah Wills has soldiers under his hands just as the greatest prince, until Pharaoh get the news and said: "Let him in", then he entered, and when he came, Pharaoh said to him: "Do I know you?" He said: Yes, "Did we not cherish thee as a child among us", Moses replied by mentioning Allah Almighty, then Pharaoh said: Take him, then Moses threw his rod, and behold! It was a serpent, plain, shown to the people and defeated, including twenty-five thousand killed each other, and Pharaoh was defeated and stands to enter the house, and said: Make a deadend between us to look at it. And Mouses replied: I was not ordered to do so, but I was ordered to combat you, and if you didn't come to me, I would enter to you, so Allah Almighty revealed to Mouses: Make a deadend between you and him and tell him to make it himself. Then Pharaoh said: Let it forty days. He did. Pharaoh come to the latrine only once every forty days, and that day has differed forty times, he said: Moses Allah be pleased with him went out of the city, and when he passed by the lion, this latter covered his tails, and went with Mouses to satisfy him, and not to provoke him, nor to any of Bani Israel.

Nouf Al Bakali narrated: "Allah has stimulated to the mountains that I'm coming down on one of you. He said: All the mountains had been high except for Mount Tabor, it humbled and said: I'm satisfied with what Allah had given to me. He said: And it was so. ***Wahb Ibn Munabbih narrated:*** Moses has asked Allah Almighty and said: Allah, what will you order me? He said: Do not associate partners with me. He said: And what? He said: And obey your mother. He said: And what? He said: And obey your mother. Wahab said: Obeying father increases work, and obeying mother sets the appointed time. ***Wahab said:*** Moses Allah be pleased with him said: O Allah, they ask me how was your start? He said: Tell them that I am above all, and I am the creator of all, and the one after all. ***Amr ibn Maymun narrated:*** Moses Allah be pleased with him saw a man on the throne and was jealous of his place and asked about him, they said: we tell you about his work, he doesn't envy people on what Allah gave them instead of him, he doesn't gossip and doesn't hinder his parents. He said: O Allah, who hinder his parents? He said: Insulting them until they insult him. ***Abu Al Jalad narrated:*** that Moses has asked Allah Almighty and said: O Allah bring down a ruling verse to guide your servants. He said: Allah revealed to Moses to go, everything that my servants want to bring to you, bring it to them. ***Abo Al Jalad narrated:*** Allah Almighty revealed to Moses Allah be pleased with him: If you

Asceticism - Part 1 -

remember me, do so and your parts shaking up, and be humbled and reassured. And if you remember me, let your tongue behind your heart. And if you stand before me, stand in the position of an abject servant, and blame yourself, it's worth to be blamed. And beg me by an afraid heart and an honest tongue. *Abo Al Jalad narrated:* Moses said: "O Allah how can I thank you and the smallest grace you have set for me do not reward my whole work, he said: he revealed to Moses, you had just thanked me. *Ka'ab Al-Ahbar narrated* that Moses Allah be pleased with him was saying in his prayer: O Allah, make my heart soft by repentance and do not make my heart as harsh as stone. *Al Mundhir heard Wahab saying:* Allah Almighty said to Moses Allah be pleased with him: Give an order to your folks to be closer to me and to pray for me in the tenth, meaning the tenth of Dhu'l-Hijjah, if the tenth day came, they would come to me to forgive them. Wahab said: And it's the day that the Jews asked for him, then they led him to sin. *Ka-ab Al-Ahbar narrated:* Allah revealed to Moses Almighty to teach goodness and learn it, I provide light to the teacher of goodness and the learner of it in their graves so as not to be afraid there. *Ka'ab narrated:* "O Allah, are you close to beg you, or far away to call you?" He said: O Moses, I am the companion of who remembered me. He said: what about being in a shameful case to remind you? He said: and what is it? He said: ritual impurity and feces. He said:

O Moses remember me, anyway. ***Qatada narrated that Moses said:*** O Allah, what is it the inferior thing that you placed on earth? He said: Justice is the inferior that I've placed on earth. ***Yahya ibn Salim Al-Taefi narrated:*** Moses Allah be pleased with him has requested Allah Almighty for something and it got difficult and he said: As Allah Wills, so then he got what he requested in his hands. And he said: O Allah, I was asking for this a long time since so and so, and you gave it to me now. He said: Allah revealed to Moses: O Moses didn't you know that your saying of As Allah Wills, brings you what you've requested. ***Yahya ibn Salim Al-Taefi narrated:*** The word that the Angels drive away the devils when they overhear, As Allah Wills. ***Ka'ab ibn Alqama narrated:*** Moses, the Prophet of Allah, Allah be pleased with him, when he ran away from Pharaoh. He said: "O Allah, advise me," He said: I advise you to not chose me for something except if you choose me instead of it, because I do not have mercy nor provision on who is not like this". He said: So, what, O Allah? He said: Your mother, she carried you in weakness upon weakness. He said: And what? He said: And your father. He said: And what? He said: To love to people what you love to yourself and hate to them what you hate for yourself. He said: And what? He said: Do not make my servants in misery, be there in their needs, you present my soul, so, I am visionary, listener, and witnessed.

Asceticism - Part 1 -

Wahab ibn Munabbih narrated: Allah Almighty gave to Moses Allah be pleased with him a glow, and Aaron said to him: give it to me, O brother, so he did. Then Aaron gave him his two sons. There was a vessel in Jerusalem that the Prophets honors it so as the kings do after them, so they were watering the wine on it. Then, a fire has come down from heaven and kidnapped Aaron's sons then went up with them, and Aaron was alarmed and rose up praying and begging. So, Allah Almighty stimulates to Aaron: That's what I do to those who disobey me from my obedience folks, so what about the ones who disobeying me from my disobedience folks! ***Mohammed ibn Al-Nudar Al Harthy narrated:*** Allah Almighty revealed to Mouses: Be awake and lover to yourself, every confident who doesn't match you on my rejoice, he is an enemy to you and harden your heart, and be one of those who remember Me in order to be worthy of reward and gets more. ***Ibn Abbas Allah be pleased with them narrated:*** Moses, peace be upon him, said: O Allah, which of your servants do you love most? He said: who remember me the most. So, he said: O Allah, which of your servants is richer? He said: The one who is satisfied with what I gave him. He said: O Allah, which of your servants is the wisest? He said: The one who judges himself by what he judges the people. ***Mujahid narrated:*** There are seventy prophets who pilgrimage Masjid

Al-Haram including Moses ibn Omran Allah be pleased with him with two cotton dresses and he was asked, then the mountains respond him. ***Imran Al-Juni narrated:*** Moses Allah be pleased with him was advising his folks, and one of his people rose up and cut his shirt, so Moses was told: Tell the owner of the shirt to do not cut his shirt to open his heart to me. ***Ammar ibn Yasser narrated*** that his companions were waiting for him when he came out, they said: What is it that let you late on us, O Prince? He said: I'm going to tell you that the one who was before you, were Moses Allah be pleased with him. He said: O Allah tell me about the people you love? He said: Why? He said: To love them. He said: A servant at the end or the edge of the earth, heard by another servant at the end of the earth who do not know him. So, if he had a misfortune, it would be as if it has hit him, and if he is hurt by a thorn, it would be as if it has hurt him, he loves him only to me, that is my lover servant. He said: O Allah, did you creature creatures to enter them to fire and torture them? So, Allah Almighty stimulates to him: They are all my creatures. Then he said: Transplant a plant, he did. He said: Water it, he did. Rise up on it, he did, As Allah Wills from that, and harvest it, and he said: What did you do with your plants, O Moses? He said: I'm done with it, and I raise it up. He said: Did you not left some of it? He said: What is not good, and what I do not need. He said: Same as I, I do not torture except for those who are not good, and for those who I do not need. ***Wahab narrated:*** I got a news that Moses Allah be pleased with him has passed by a man praying and begging and said: O Allah, have mercy on him, Allah Almighty revealed to Mouses: If he prayed me until his strength cut off, I would not respond him until he saw my right on him. ***Wahb ibn Munabbih narrated:*** Allah Almighty revealed to Mouses Allah be pleased with him: Your folks build me houses and close me sacrifices, and I do not live in houses, nor eat meat, but a portion between me and them to adjust between the richer and the poorer, and a portion between me and them if they pleased the poorer, I'm pleased, and if they annoyed them, I'm annoyed. ***Wahb ibn Munabbih narrated:*** Moses said to the Israelites: Bring me the goodness man of yours. They bring him a man and said: Are you the goodness man of Israelites? He said: That's what they said. He said: Bring me the wickedness of them, he said: He went and came back and none with him. He said: Did you bring to me their wickedness? He said: I know none of them what I know of myself. He said: You are their goodness. ***Wahab ibn Munabbih narrated:*** Moses Allah be pleased with him said: O Allah, which of your servants do you love? He said: The one who remembered me. He said: O Allah, which of your servants do you love? He said: Those who visit the sick, and comfort the bereaved and accompany a funeral procession. ***At'aa narrated:***

Moses has circumambulated the Ka'aba, and in between Safa and Marwa, and he was saying: O Allah here I come. So, Allah Almighty responded to him: O Moses, here I come, here I am, and he has a Jubbah of wool. **Anas ibn Malik narrated** that the prophet peace be upon him said: I passed one night by Moses Allah be pleased when he was praying on his grave. ***Ata ibn Yasar narrated:*** Moses said: O Allah, who is your family who you will keep them under your throne? He said: Who their hands are clear, and who their hearts are pure, and who they fall in love on me, and who if I remembered, they remember too, and if they remember, I do remember them, and who do full ablution in hardship, and get back to me just as the birds get back to their nest, they adore me just as a boy adores people, and get angry with my fighters if they are as bad as the tiger gets angry if he fights. ***Wahab ibn Munabbih narrated:*** We get a news that Allah Almighty said to Moses Allah be pleased with him: O Moses, with my pride and honor, if the soul that you killed gave me a blink of an eye, and I'm its Creator or Provider, I will taste you the torture, but I forgive you about it, it did not give me the blink of an eye, and I'm its Creator and Provider. ***Umaran al-Qusayr and narrated:*** Moses ibn Imran said: "O Allah, when should I asked for you?" He said: Asked for me when the hearts are broken, I stand with them in the selling day, otherwise they do not destroy. ***Thabit narrated:*** When Moses ibn Amran Allah

Asceticism - Part 1 -

be pleased with him died, angels were circumambulated in heaven and said: Moses died, no soul does not die. ***Abu Umaran Al-Jouni narrated:*** that Moses Allah be pleased with him when death came to him, he grieved and then said: I am not afraid to die, but I am afraid that my tongue would stop remembering Allah Almighty when I'm dying. He said: Moses had three daughters, and he said: "O my daughters, the Israelites will offer you this world, so do you not accept it to get heaven."

Dawud – David- asceticism (Peace be upon him)

Abdullah ibn Al-Mohajer narrated: That the Prophet (peace and blessings of Allah be upon him) used to abhor the multitude of tears. He said: "let me cry before the day of weeping." Before the bones are burned, and the beard flames, before I am commanded by angels that are stoning, they do not disobey God, and do what they are commanded'. *Al-Hassan narrated:* The Prophet of God Dawud, may God bless him and grant him peace, said: "My God, if every hair of mine has two tongues glorifying at day and night, and all the days, indeed no blessing will be gone'. Dawud (peace be upon him) said: "O Lord, is one of you creature tonight remembers you longer than me?'. So,

God, Almighty, said to him: Yes, the frog, and Allah has said his verse: Work ye, sons of Dawud, with thanks! but few of My servants are grateful! He said: O Lord, how can I thank you and you who give me blessings? You give me the blessing of grace, and then increased grace with grace Blessings and gratefulness from you Lord so, how can I thank you Lord?' He said: Now you know me, Dawud, indeed'. ***Al-Ja'ed narrated:*** Dawud (peace be upon him) said: "O Lord, what is the reward of condoling a sad person seeking only your face wants? He said: His reward is that he wore the garment of piety. He said: My God, what is the reward of someone who made a funeral seeking only your face? He said: His reward is that his funeral shall be raised by my angels if he dies, and that I pray for his soul in life. He said: My God, what is the reward of someone who supports an orphan or a widow? He said that His reward is that his shadow is under my throne on the day of no shadow but my shadow. ***Al Ja'ed said: I asked my father Othman:*** what is the meaning "Asnad"? He said: that he seeks only your face. He said:" my God said what the reward of someone who his eyes are full of tears from your fear? He said: his reward is that I would secure him on the Day of the Great Fears, and that I would protect his face from Hell'. ***Malik narrated:*** Dawud (peace be upon him) said: Oh God make my love towards you more than my love to myself, my hearing, my sight, my family

Asceticism - Part 1 -

and the cold water'. ***Al Jariri narrated:*** Dawud (peace be upon him) asked Jibril: 'O Jibril, which night is better? He said: O Dawud, I know only that the throne shakes from magic'. ***Al Obeid ibn Omeir narrated:*** Dawud (peace be upon him): A kindergarten grew around him from his tears, and Allah, Almighty, revealed to him: "O Dawud, you want me to increase your wealth and your sons?" He said, "Any Lord, I want to forgive me. He said: O God, please forgive my sins'. ***Sa'd ibn Monabbah narrated; when*** Dawud (peace be upon him) committed a sin, he did not have food except mixed with the tears of his eyes and did not drink any drink except mixed with the tears of his eyes'. ***Omar ibn Abdel Rahman narrated:*** I heard Sa'd ibn Monabbah telling Dawud: " O Lord, I cannot bear over the heat of your sun, so how can bear your hot fire ! O Lord, I cannot bear the voice of your mercy, I mean thunder, how can I bear the voice of your torment'. ***Abdullah ibn Abo Malika narrated:*** Dawud (peace be upon him): 'O Lord, get me away from bad people, not to be a bad man'. Abdul Rahman ibn Dorba narrated: I was informed that Dawud (peace be upon him) invokes God saying: O Allah, do not make me poor, so not to forget, and do not make me rich, so not to transgress'. ***Abo Omran El-Gony narrated*** said this verse: 'And has the news of the litigants reached you? When they climbed over the wall into (his) Mihrab (private chamber of worship); When they entered in upon Dawud, he was terrified of them'. They said: "climbed over the wall to reach Dawud, then he was terrified of them'." They said: "Fear not! (We are) two litigants, one of us has wronged the other, therefore judge between us with truth, and treat us not with injustice, and guide us to the right way. He said to them: 'Sit on the enemies' seat, then they sit on the enemies' seat. He said to them: 'tell the story'. One of them said: 'Verily, this my brother (in religion) has ninety-nine ewes, while I have (only) one ewe, and he says: "Hand it over to me, and he overpowered me in speech. He said, Dawud exclaimed and said: "He has wronged you in demanding your ewe in addition to his ewes. And, verily, many partners oppress one another". He said: Then one he said to him, "O Dawud, you deserve to have your head knocked with a stick and go up, and Dawud knows that he has rebuked his sin." He said, "He docked in his place forty days and nights, he does not raise his head except for obligatory prayer". He said: Until he dried, and bleed his forehead, his neck and knees. He said: then an angel came to him and said: O Dawud, I am the messenger of your Lord to you, and he says to you, lift your head, I have forgiven you. And he said: How then, Lord, you are fair judge, and you are the Dianne of religion, you don't pass on aggression of a brute. How can you forgive my aggression?! "He said:" Then he left what Allah wanted and then another angel came to him. He said: O Dawud , I am the messenger of your Lord to you. And he says to you, "You are coming to me on the Day of Judgment when you and the son of Suria are soliciting for me, and I will judge him against you and then ask him to give it to me, so he does. The, I gave him from Paradise to plead and then forgive him. He said: Now I know, Lord, that you have forgiven me'. **Abdel Rahman ibn Bozareya narrated:** there are three letters in the Psalms of the family of Dawud : Blessed is he who did not follow the path of sinners and blessed is he who did not follow the command of the oppressors. Al Hassan narrated: Dawud (peace be upon him) said: O God, what is the best blessing? He said: The fruit of your hand, Dawud . **Abo Abdullah Al-Jadaly narrated: God revealed to** Dawud (peace be upon him) this verse: "O Dawud , Love Me and My lovers and endear Me to My servants." Dawud said, "O my Lord! I love You and Your lovers, but how shall I endear You to Your servants?" He said, "Remember Me before them (excessively), for sure they will remember Me not but only with good." **Moslama narrated:** Dawud (peace be upon him) said: "O God, how can I thank you and I do not come to thank you except by your grace?! "God revealed to Dawud:" Dawud , do not you know that the blessings you have are from me? "He said:" Yes, any Lord, "he said:" I hope that you thank me for that'. **Abo Omran Al-Gony narrated:** "God revealed to Dawud :"O Dawud, warn my servants of the righteous, so they do not admire themselves, and do not trust in their deeds; for none of my servants will be appointed for account, and I will apply my justice on him, and I tortured him without oppressing him. And promise the sinners that there is not a fault that is big for me to forgive and skip'. ***Abo Al-Galad narrated*** that Dawood the Prophet (peace be upon him) commanded to pray : Pray in Group. Then, people came out and they saw that it would be a day of exhortation, chastisement and du'aa '. Then he said, "O God, forgive us." And left. The latter met the first and they said: what happened? They said: the Prophet (peace be upon him) called only for one prayer and then he left. They said: Praise be to Allah. We were hoping that this day would be a day of worship, prayer, exhortation and discipline, so he called upon only one prayer. They said: "And Allah has revealed to him to your people informed me that they belittled your prayers. He who I forgive, I set his life and hereafter right for him". ***Khaled ibn Thabet Al-Rab'ey narrated: I found in the beginning of*** Psalms which refers to Psalms of Dawud (peace be upon him): The head of wisdom is the fear of the Lord Almighty. ***Ibn Abbas (peace be upon him) narrated:*** "God revealed to Dawud: "Say to the oppressors not to remember me, I really have to remember those who remembered me, and I mention them by cursing them'. ***Abo Al Salilak narrated:*** The Prophet Dawud (peace be upon him) enters the mosque and sees a gathering of Israeli

Asceticism - Part 1 -

group and sits close to them, they says: "O Poor people". Ayoub Al Falastini narrated: It is written in the psalms of Dawood (peace be upon him): Do you know who I forgive from my servants? He said: Who, O Lord? He said, "to whom once committed a sin, So his joints trembled, who I commanded my angels not to write that sin upon him". **Hisham ibn Orwa narrated that his father said:** Dawud, peace be upon him, made the basket from the wicker while standing on the altar, then he sent it to the market to sell it, and eat from its return". *Ta'ma Al-Ja'fary narrated:* Dawud, peace be upon him, asked his God, Almighty, to show him his companion on people of the earth, so Allah, Almighty, revealed to him: go to such village and find who is doing so and so, that's your companion. He went to the village and asked about him and he was led to him. He found him a man who brings wood, cut it into cane, tie a bundle and goes to the market and says: who buys good things, I will cut them with my hand and carry him on my back'. *Abdel Rahman ibn Ibzy narrated:* Dawud, peace be upon him, was the most patient, the most kind, and the most who can block his anger'. *Sa'eed ibn AbdelAziz narrated:* Dawud, peace be upon him, said: O Lord, how do I seek you in the earth with advice? He said: remember me a lot, love those who love me from the black and white, judge between people as you judge on yourself and avoid backbiting'. *Sa'eed ibn Hilal narrated:* Dawud, peace be upon him, used to visit his companions and they think he is sick, and he was only afraid from God Almighty. **Kays ibn Abbad narrated:** Dawud, peace be upon him, invokes and says: O Lord, I ask you for a companion who helps me if I remember you, and who reminds me if I forget you. O Lord, I seek refuge in you from a companion who does not help me if I remember you, and who does not remind me if I forget you. O Lord, if I passed a people that are remembering you, and wanted to skip them, then break my legs which passes them so that I sit with them and remember you'. **Abo Sa'd Al-Mo'adab narrated** about a man that said: Dawud, peace be upon him, said: Oh God, do not make me corrector alluring, then disregard my living and disbelieve in your grace. **Abo Yazid narrated:** Dawud, peace be upon him, would prolong the prayer, then bow down, then lift his head and says, "I have lifted my head to you, who flourishes heaven. The slaves look to their lords, O inhabitant of heaven'. **Abo Al-Hassan narrated:** Dawud, peace be upon him, was saying: Oh God, there is no sickness that exhausts me, nor health that makes me forget you, but those between them'. **Yazid ibnn Rabe'a narrated: Dawud,** peace be upon him, looked at sickle of fire falling between heaven and earth and said: O Lord, what is this? He said: "This is my curse, I will bring it into the house of every oppressor." **Awn Al-Madiny narrated: I heard one of our companions saying: God, Almighty, revealed to**

Asceticism - Part 1 -

Dawud, peace be upon him, I have sent down appetencies to earth on the weak of my servants, not to the heroes'. ***Thabet narrate*** : Dawud, peace be upon him, has divided hours of day & night on his family, that there came not an hour of the night and day, but a man of the family of Dawud is praying'. He said: Allah, Almighty, revealed this verse to them: "Work ye, sons of David, with thanks! but few of My servants are grateful!" ***Ibn Sohayb narrated:*** Dawud, peace be upon him, was invoking to Allah saying: Glory to Allah who is the extractor of thanksgiving by granting, and extractor of the invoking by calamity'. ***Al Awza'ey narrated: God, Almighty, revealed to*** Dawud, peace be upon him, saying: O Dawud, Do not I teach you two things if you do them to make people's faces accustomed to you, and reach my satisfaction? He said: Yes, Lord. He said: hold between me and you by pious, and interfere with people by their morals'. Mohamed ibn Gahada narrated: ***God, Almighty, revealed to*** Dawud, peace be upon him, saying: It is the wrongdoers of remembering me, and sitting in my mosques, I made myself - or imposed on myself - that I remember who remembers me, and if the oppressor remembers me, I will curse him'.

• CHAPTER 10 •

Soliman Ascetism (Peace be upon him)

Soliman ibn Dawood (peace be upon him) said: "we have given what people were given and what were not given , and we learned what people had learned and did not learn. We did not find anything better than three words: the dream in anger and satisfaction, the intention in poverty and richness, and the fear of God in secret and public. *Soliman ibn Dawood peace be upon him narrated:* we tried to live in its softness and severances, and we found the minimum of it would suffice. *Wahab ibn Monabbah narrated:* My father told me: " Soliman ibn Dawood (peace be upon him) had a thousand houses with flasks from the above and iron from below. He carried the wind one day, and he passed by a ploughman. The ploughman looked at him and said: the family of Dawood were given a great king, and the wind carried his words, and put it in the ears of Soliman (peace be upon him). He said: he went down until the ploughman came then said: I heard your words, but I walked to you, lest you wish what you cannot afford, since one praise accepted by God is better than what I have given to family of Dawood. The ploughman said: I pray that Allah take away your grief as you took away my grief". *It was narrated that Yahya ibn Abi Katheer said:* Soliman ibn Dawood (peace be upon him) said to his son: "My son, do not be jealous of your family, then they will be afflicted by evil, if they are innocent, my son weakness is from modesty, and from it comes the reverence of God Almighty. My son If you want to anger your enemy, do not lift the stick from your son. O my son, as the wedge enters between the two stones, and as the snake enters between the two stones, also the sin enters between the two sellers". *Katada said that Soliman (peace be upon him said):* Amazingly how does the merchant sell? Swear in the morning and sleep at night. *Malik narrated that Soliman ibn Dawood said to his son,* "follow lion and lions, and don't follow a woman". *Bakr ibn Abdellah narrated* that Dawood said to Soliman (peace be upon them): Which is colder, which is sweeter, which is closer, which is farthest, which is the least, which is the most, which is most friendly, and which is the most thing causes loneliness? he said: The best thing is the Spirit of God among His slaves, and the coldest thing is pardon of God Almighty for His slaves and the forgiveness of the slaves to each other, the most friendly is the soul inside the body, the most lonely is the body without soul, the least thing certainty, and the most thing is suspicion, the closest thing is the Hereafter in the world, and the farthest thing is the world from the Hereafter or as he said: that Yahya said, Soliman (Peace be upon him) said to his son: "My son, you must fear God Almighty, it's above everything". **Chahr ibn Hawcheb narrated**: The angel of death entered to Soliman, so he kept looking at a man who is constantly looking at him. When he came out, the man said: who is this? He said: This is the angel of death, peace be upon him, he said: "I saw him looking at me as if he wants me. He said: What do you want? He said, "I was looking forward to the capture of his soul in India. He said to him: 'I want that the wing lifts me and throw me in Hind. He said: he called for the wind, he was lifted on it and throw him in Hind. The angel of death came to Soliman (peace be upon him) and said to him: you were constantly looking to a man who was sitting with me? He said: I was wondering about him, I was ordered to take his soul in Hind when he is at your place". **Khaythama narrated:** The angel of death entered to Soliman when he was with a friend. Soliman said to him: why you come to the family of the house and take their souls, and let the family of the house and don't take any of their souls? He said: I do not know whose soul I take, I am under the throne and a written order are given to me with names. **Yahya ibn Abi Katheer narrated** that Soliman ibn Dawood (peace be upon him) said to his son: O son, how ugly is the sin with the abominations, and how ugly the misguidance with the guidance, and how ugly is so and so, and what is the uglier than this man who was a slave and left the worship of his Lord. **Ibn Ataa narrated** that his father said: Soliman (peace be upon him) used to make the wickers by his hand, eats the barley bread with the nun and feeds Bani of Israel. **Yehia narrated:** Soliman said to his son: O my son, beware of slander it's like sword's edge".

Abo Al-Sedeek Al Naji narrated: Soliman ibn Dawood(peace be upon him) went out to people invoking Allah for rain, he passed by an ant lying on its back raising its legs to the sky saying: O God, we are of your creatures that have no dispense over your provisions, either you give us water or to destroy us, Soliman said to the people: Return, you have been given water because of the prayer of others". **Abdullah ibn Amr ibn Al-Aas narrated:** I heard the Prophet of Allah (peace be upon him) saying: Soliman ibn Dawood (peace be upon him) asked God for three things, and he gave him two, and we hope that you give him the third. He asked him for a decision which met his decision, then he gave it to him. He asked him for a dominion that will not be given to anyone after him, then he gave it to

Asceticism - Part 1 -

him, and he asked him about a man who came out of his house, seeking only to pray in this mosque, he is taken out of his sin like the day his mother gave his birth. We hope that Allah Almighty has given it to him.

• CHAPTER 11 •

Loqman Ascetism (Peace be upon him)

Ibn Katheer[1], in his book "The Beginning and the End in History", narrates a complete text in his translation of the story of Luqman (peace be upon him) from the book of asceticism to Imam Ahmad ibn Hanbal, which is fully consistent with the manuscript that is in our hands. In this text, there is no doubt that this text is the chapter of the article in the ratio of the book of asceticism to Ahmed ibn Hanbal, which is a distinction between uncertainty and uncertainty, in which suspicion is raised regarding how much it's not attributed to him, it is worth recording this text, which Ibn Katheer on many pages of this book.

---

[1] Ibn Katheer is well known Islamic scholar came after Imam Ahmad by centuries, it is added here as reference.

Asceticism - Part 1 -

Ibn Katheer says: Imam Ahmad mentioned for him (Luqman) in the book of asceticism a translation which narrated many important benefits, and said:

Mujahid narrated: (We have given the wisdom to Luqman), he said: Jurisprudence and correctness in the absence of prophecy. ***Ibn Abbas narrated:*** Luqman was a Habashi slave". ***Sa'ed ibn Al-Massib narrated*** that Luqman was a tailor. ***Malik - ibn Dinar - narrated***: Luqman said to his son" My son, take obedience to God as a trade, profits come to you without goods". ***Muhammad ibn Wasie*** narrated: Luqman says to his son: "My son, fear Allah, and do not show people that you fear Allah to honor you, while your heart is vain". ***Khalid Al-Ruba'I narraed:*** Luqman was a Habashi slave and a carpenter. His lord said to him, "Slay me a sheep," and he slaughtered a sheep for him. He said: bring me the sweetest two chews in it. He brought him the tongue and heart, and I ordered you to receive the worst of the chewing, and I gave the tongue and the heart. And I ordered you to throw the worst two chews in it, then you threw the tongue and heart. He said to him: It is nothing better than them if they are good, and nothing worse than them if they are vicious".

Al Ja'd Abo Othman narrated: that Luqman said to his son: do not seek the love of ignorant not to think you are satisfied with his work, and do not underestimate the sage, so he loses the desire to have it in you".

Abdullah ibn Zayd narrated: Luqman said: "The hand of God is on the mouths of the wise. No one of them speaks except with what God wants him to say". **Ibn Jare'h narrated:** I put mask on my head at night". Omar said to me: didn't you know that Loqman said: mask in the day is a humiliation". Or he said- a miracle at night. So, why do you mask your head at night? He said: I said to him: Lukman did not have a debt". **Sofiane narrated:** Luqman said to his son, "My son, don't regret silence ever, if the words are made of silver, then silence is made of gold". **Qatada ibn Loqman narrated:** stay away from the evil, it will stay away from you. The evil is created for evil." **Hisham ibn Erwa narrated** about his father and said: It is written in wisdom my son beware of desire, since desire dismisses near from near, and removes the rule as it removes the raging, my son beware of the extreme anger, the extreme anger destroys the heart of the wise person". *It was narrated that Ubayd ibn 'Umeir said:* Luqman said to his son as he preached him: "O my son, choose the councils very carefully. If you find them remembering God Almighty, sit with them, if you are a scholar, your knowledge will benefit you, and if you are stupid, they will teach you. God might give you mercy that afflicts you when you are with them. O son, don't sit in the council that does not mention God, if you are a scholar, your knowledge will not benefit you, and if you are stupid, they will increase your stupidity. God might give you indignation that afflicts you when you are with them. O my son, don't envy lords whose arms are wide and kill those who believe in God. God keeps a slaughter for him that never dies"

Hisham ibn Erwa narrated about his father: It is written in wisdom: "O son, let your speech be good, and let your face be simple, you will be beloved to people than who gives them provisions". He said: It is written in Wisdom or in Testament: Mercy is the top of wisdom. He said: it's written in testament: as you provide mercy, you will be given mercy". He said: it's written in Wisdom: love your friend and friend of your father".

Abo Qelaba narrated: it was said to Loqman: which people are most patient? He said: patience that is not followed by harm. It was said: Who are the people who have the most knowledge? He said: who adds from people's knowledge to his knowledge. It was said: which people are the best? He said: the rich". It was said richness from money? He said: No - but the rich who has the good when it's sought, otherwise he dispensed himself from people".

Sofian - the son of Oyayna – narrated: it was said to Loqman: who are the evillest? He said: who does not care if people see him as abusive. **Malik ibn Dinar narrated:** I found in some Wisedom: God destroys the bones of those who are talking with people's desires". I found also in it: You have no good In learning what you do not know, and in working with what you have learned, such as a man who cut wood and packed a pack, then failed to carried it, then he joined anther one to it".

Abu Sa'eed narrated: Luqman said to his son: "My son, let only the pious eat your food, and consult scholars in your matter"." This is the sum of what Imam Ahmad said in these places. We have been presented to many affects they did not see. He mentioned also things we don't have, God knows. **Muhammad ibn Jihdah narrated:** Loqman said: "It will come a time when the sight of a wise person is not acknowledged." **Sofian narrated:** Luqman Al-Hakim said to his son: "O son, the world is a deep sea, where many people have sunk. So, make pious to Allah Almighty your ship in this world. And it's fill belief in God Almighty, and its sail is entrusting in God Almighty, so you will be rescued". **Al Hassan narrated:** Loqman said to his son: "My son, I lifted rock and iron, I found nothing is heavier than vicious neighbor". **Mohamed ibn Wase' narrated:** "My son, do not show people that you fear God while your heart is vicious". **O'of narrated:** Loqman said to his son: "O son, the believer has two hearts, a heart that he hopes with, and a heart that fears with. **'Abd-Allaah ibn Dinar narrated:** Luqman said to his son: "My son, put yourself down in a place –

Asceticism - Part 1 -

from your Lord – for who is not in a need for you, and where you did not change". My son be like those who don't seek thanking from people, not to gain their hatred, his soul will be exhausted, and people will be restful from him". Al-Seri ibn Yehia narrated: Luqman said to his son: "My son, wisdom has placed the poor in the seats of the kings*". **Kitab ibn Kalaba narrated:** Luqman was told: who is the most knowledgeable? He said: who adds from people's knowledge to his knowledge. He said: who is the richest? He said: who is satisfied with what h had been given. He said: who has the best virtue? He said: the rich believer. people said: "from money?" He said: No, but from knowledge, if they needed him, they found knowledge with him, and if he is not needed did not need, he dispense himself". **Abo Al-Hakam narrated:** it was said to Loqman: what is your wisdom? He said: that I don't ask about what is sufficient for me, and don't interfere in what is not in my business. **Mo'aweya ibn Quora narrated:** Loqman said to his son: My son, sit with the good from God's worshipers, you will get the good from their amenities. It might be at the end that Mercy falls upon them, so you will be afflicted by it". My son, don't sit with the evils, you will not get any good from their companion. It might be at the end that a punishment falls upon them, so you will be punished as well". **Abo Najah narrated:** Loqman means: Silence is wisdom and little who are doing it".

'Auf ibn Abdullah narrated: Luqman said to his son: "urge Allah Almighty for something that doesn't secure you from his canniness, and fear from God so that you are not desperate from his mercy. He said: O father, how can I do that while I have just one heart? He said: "My son, the believer has two hearts, a heart with which he desires, and a heart with which he fears". Abo Othman- Sheikh of the people of Basra - narrated that Luqman said to his son: My son, do not seek the love of ignorant not to think you are satisfied with his work, and do not underestimate the wise, so he loses the desire to have it in you". **Abd-Allah ibn Dinar said:** Lukman came from a journey and his young man came in the way and said, "What did my father do?" He said: "He died." He said, "Praise be to Allah. You own my staff'. He said: "What did my mother do?" He said: she died. He said: my grief has gone. He said: "What did my wife do?" He said, "she died". He said: renew my bed". He said: "What did my sister do?" He said, "She died". He said: she did my private part". He said: "What did my brother do?" He said, "He died". He said: my back is broken". **Muhammad Al-Makki narrated:** Loqman said to his son: "O my son, sit with the scholars and cowd them with your knees, for Allah Almighty revives hearts with the light of wisdom, as He gives life to the dead earth with the heavy rain from of the sky".

CHAPTER 12

Jesus asceticism (Peace be upon him)

Wahb ibn Monabbah narrated: If you are guided by the people of affliction, know that you are guided by the path of the prophets and the righteous, and If you are guided by the people of prosperity, then know that he has taken a path for you that is not in their path, and has left you out of their path". **Ja'far Abo Ghalib narrated:** this speech has been reported to be included in the legacy of Jesus ibn Maryam (peace be upon him): O Messenger of the Apostles love God, Almighty by the hatred of the people of sin and approached him by hating them and seek his satisfaction with your anger from them. They said: O Prophet of God, who shall we sit with? "He said:" sit with those whose logic increases your work, who reminds you with Allah once meeting them, and whose actions leads to your asceticism in life". ***Malik ibn Dinar narrated:*** O 'Jesus, preach to yourself, if you are preached, preach to people, otherwise feel ashamed from me". ***Wahb ibn Monabbah narrated:*** Jesus ibn Maryam (peace be upon him) was standing on a grave and with him the Apostles or said: In a group of his companions, said: The owner of the grave inside, he said: Remember me in the darkness of the grave, its brutality and narrowness: Jesus (peace be upon him) said: You have been in a narrower place inside the wombs of your mothers! If God, Almighty, wished the to expand it, he would do that". ***Wahb ibn Monabbah was heard saying:*** Jesus said: increase your remembrance of Allah, Almighty, his praise, consecration, and obey him. It's enough of one when praying if God, Almighty, is satisfied with him to say: O God forgive my sin, set my life right for me and relieve me of the misfortunes, my God". ***Salem ibn Abo Al-Ja'ed narrated:*** Jesus (peace be upon him) said: He is blessed who kept his tongue, and his house was large enough for him, and cried from the remembrance of his sin". ***Khaythama narrated:*** Jesus (peace be upon him) said: Blessed is the believer, and then Blessed is He, who preserves God Almighty and his Son after Him! ". ***Hilal ibn Yasar narrated:*** Jesus (peace be upon him) was saying: "If one of you gave charity with his right hand, let him hide it from his left hand, and if he prays, let him be close to his door. Allah Almighty divides the praise as he divides the blessing." ***Abo***

Asceticism - Part 1 -

Thamama Al-Saydi narrated: Apostles said to Jesus ibn Maryam: Who is the sincere to God Almighty? He said: Whoever works for Allah and does not like to be praised by people. They said: Who is the advisor of Allah? He said: Whoever begins with the right of God then prefers the right of God than the right of the people and if he is presented to two issues, one for life and other for the Hereafter, he begins with the issue of the Hereafter and devote to the order of the world afterwards". ***Thabet narrated:*** it was said to Jesus ibn Maryam: O Messenger of God, if you take a donkey you ride for your need? He said: I am honored to God that he will not make something occupying me concerns from him". ***Abo Al-Jalad narrated:*** Jesus (peace be upon him) said to Apostles: Verily, I say to you: What do you want, the world, or the Hereafter? They said: O Messenger of God, explain to us this matter, we would see that we want one of them? He said: If you want the world, then you obey the Lord of the world, who has the keys of its coffers in his hand, and if you want the Hereafter, then obey the Lord of the Hereafter, who owns it and shall give it to you, but you want neither this nor that". ***Abo Al-Jalad narrated:*** Jesus ibn Maryam (peace be upon him) advised the Apostles: Do not talk too much without mentioning Allah Almighty not to harden your hearts, and whose heart is hard is away from God Almighty, but he is not aware of that, and do not look at the sins of people as if you were the lords but you look at your sins as if you are slaves, and the people are two kinds of men: healed and afflicted and have mercy on the afflicted people for their affliction and thank God for wellness". ***Yazid ibn Maysara narrated:*** Jesus ibn Maryam (peace be upon him) said: Why do I not see the best worship in you? They said: What is the best worship, O Spirit of God? He said: Modesty to God Almighty". ***Ibrahem Al-Taymi narrated:*** Make your treasures in heaven, the heart of one is at his treasure". ***Abo Al Hathil narrated:*** I heard a monk saying: The devil said to Jesus, peace be upon him, when he placed on Jerusalem, he said: I thought you revive the dead! If you can do so, ask God to return bread to this mountain, Jesus, peace be upon him, said to him: Are all people eat bread? ! The devil said to him: If you are as you say then retard from this place, the angels will meet you, he said: My God, Almighty ordered me not to try things to myself, I do not know whether it will be safe for or not". ***Bakr ibn Abdullah narrated:*** The Apostles lost their Prophet, peace be upon him, so they went out to search for him. He said:" They found him walking on the water. Some of them said: O Prophet of God, shall we walk to you? He said: Yes, he said: and put his leg then went to put the other then he plunged. He said: " Give me your hand, who has short faith, if the son of Adam has the weight of a grain or an atom of certainty then he would walk on the water".

Asceticism - Part 1 -

Hilal ibn Yasaf narrated: Jesus ibn Maryam (peace be upon him) says: If one of you fasts, then leave his beard and wipe his lips until he goes out to the people then they say: "He is not fasting. ***Al Sha'by narrated:*** Jesus ibn Maryam (peace be upon him) says: "Charity is not to be good to who did good to you, but it is a reward for good, rather charity is to be good to those who offended you". ***Al Dabi narrated:*** A woman said to Jesus (peace be upon him) when he makes from what has been given and mocked to him "Blessed is the belly who held you , blessed is a breast that fed you," Jesus came close to her and said to her: "Blessed who has read the Book of Allah, and follow what is in it". ***Khaythama narrated:*** A woman said to Jesus (peace be upon him): "Blessed is a breast that fed you, blessed is a rock that held you," Jesus said: "Blessed who has read the Book of Allah, and follow what is in it". ***Wahb ibn Monabbah narrated:*** God revealed to Jesus, peace be upon him, this verse: O Jesus, I have given you the love of the poor, and mercy on them, love them, and they love you, and they accept you as Imam and leader, and you accept them as companions and followers, and they are two morals. know that who have them when he meets Me, he meets Me with the best deeds and most beloved to Me". ***Sophian narrated:*** when Jesus, peace be upon him, mentioned the Hour (Resurrection) he shouted and said: The son of Maryam should not silent when the Hour is mentioned to him".

Ibn Jad'aan narrated: at your service, your servant, the son of your nation and the daughter of your servant and before that Seventy Khatami prophet, their animals with fiber until they reached the mosque of the shame". ***Makhoul narrated:*** Jesus ibn Maryam said: O Apostles, who amongst you can build a house on the wave of the sea? They said: O Spirit of God and who can do that?! He said: Beware of the world, do not take a decision ". Ibn Amr narrated: Jesus ibn Maryam (peace be upon him) was saying: Truly I say to you that eating wheat bread, drinking fresh water and sleeping on a garbage with dogs is great for those who want to inherit paradise". ***Zeyad Abo Omar narrated:*** I was informed that Jesus ibn Maryam said: It is not of your benefit to learn what you did not learn and to do what you have learned. Too much knowledge increases arrogance if you do not do it". Abo Ishaq narrated: said: I was informed that Jesus ibn Maryam said: The era revolves around three days: yesterday is past preached on it, today when provided you, tomorrow you do not know what you have in it. Issues revolve on three: an issue that its adolescence is shown to you, then you follow it, and an issue that its seduction, then you avoid it". ***Abo Hilal narrated:*** Jesus ibn Maryam said: Ask me! My heart is soft, and I'm small in myself". Jesus ***Thawr ibn Yazid narrated:*** (peace be upon him) said: "Whoever learns, works, and knows, that is called great in the kingdom of heaven". ***Al Hadrami***

Asceticism - Part 1 -

narrated: He said to him that Jesus was told: "How do we walk on water?" He said: "with certainty" he said: "He was told" We are certain! " He said: "Have you considered the stones, the towns and the gold same to you?" They said: "No," he said: I think he said: "They are same to me ". ***Sa'eed ibn Abo Sa'eed Al-Makbary narrated:*** A man came to Jesus, the son of Maryam, and said, "Teacher of good, teach me something you have learned, and I am ignorant of, and benefit me and do not harm you," he said: What is it? He said: How can a person really be pious to God, Almighty? He said: it's easy; really love God from your heart, and work for him with your majesty and strength as you can and treat your species with your mercy yourself". He said: Teacher of good, and who are the sons of my species? He said: "All sons of Adam, and do not bring them what you do not like to come to you, you are truly pious to God". ***Khaythama narrated:*** Jesus (peace be upon him) made food for his companions and then invited them, then he stood and said to them: "So do them with the villages". ***Khaked Al-Hetha' narrated:*** when the messengers of Jesus ibn Maryam (peace be upon him) went to give life to the dead. "He was telling them: 'Say this, say so, and if you feel shake and tears, pray at this moment". ***Abdullah narrated:*** The prophets were milking the sheep, riding the donleys and wearing wool". ***Wahb ibn Monabbah narrated:*** Jesus ibn Maryam said to the apostles:

"Truly I say to you, and Jesus often said: 'I say to you truly that the most beloved of the world is the most appalling of the calamity". Wahab narrated: The Apostles said: O Jesus, who are the guardians of Allah Almighty who have no fear upon nor they become sad? Jesus ibn Maryam said: Those who looked into the depths of the world when people looked at its appearance, and those who looked at the future when people looked at the immediate world, then they killed in it what they feared to kill them, and left what they knew would leave them, then their Begrudging

became abatement, and their remembering of it became missing it, and their joy became sadness. They rejected who opposed them from obtainers and put away who opposed them against its rise without right and put them. The world was created at them and they did not renew it, and was destroyed between them, and they did not construct, and it died in their chests and did not revive it, they destroy it and build their Hereafter. They sell it and purchase what remains for them. They rejected it then they became happy. They saw the dead people, so they felt same punishment. They loved the mention of death, killed the mention of life. They love God and love remembering him. They illuminate with his light and illuminate by it. They give wonderful news and have wonderful news., The Book was raised by them, and they were raised by it. The Book spoke by them, and they spoke by it. The Book knew about them and they knew about it. They do not see an obtainer amongst what they obtained, nor safety without hope, nor fear without what they avoid". **Hisham Al-Destwa'y narrated:** in the insight of Jesus ibn Maryam (peace be upon him): You work for the world, while you are given provisions without work, and you do not work for the Hereafter, while you are not given provisions except by work. The bad scholars judge! You take the reward and loose the work. You are about to go out from the world to the darkness of the grave and its narrowness. God Almighty forbids you from sins and ordered you to pray and fast. So, how the people of knowledge in his world are better for him than his Hereafter while he is the best desire in the world? How to be of the scholars of his fate to the Hereafter while he is going to his life? And what is harmful to him most desired than what benefits him? How are there amongst the people of knowledge those who deny his provisions and degrade his grade while he knows it's from the knowledge of God, Almighty and His ability? How are there amongst the people of knowledge those who accuse God in his righteousness? How are there amongst the people of knowledge those who ask for words to tell them and not to work by them?". **Thabet Al-Banany narrated**: We heard that the devil appeared to Yahya ibn Zakariah, peace be upon them, and he saw him abhorrent of all things, Yahya said: O devil what these abhorrent that I see on you? He said: These are the desires with which the sons of Adam were afflicted, Yehia, peace be upon him, said: Do I have anything from it? He said: No. He said: Do they afflict me by anything? He said: Maybe you are satisfied so they made you slow in your prayer and mentioning God. He said: Is there anything else? He said: "No, he said: "There is no harm, I never feel satisfied". *Al Hussein narrated:* Yehia & Jesus (peace be upon them) met each other, Jesus said: Ask forgiveness for me, O Yahya .. You are better than me. Said Yahya: Ask forgiveness for me, O Jesus, you are better than me. Jesus said: you are better than me . I am consent with myself and God is consent with you". *Sa'ed ibn Jaber narrated:* When Yahya (peace be upon him) was killed, some of his companions said to him: "Send me the shirt of Prophet Yahya to smell it, I know that I am killed". He said: he sent it to him to find its full of fiber". *Abo Al-Hathel narrated:* A man who had committed adultery came to Jesus, peace be upon him, man and he ordered them to throw him with stone. He said to them, "A man who committed same action shall not throw him with stone. They dropped stones from their hands, except Yahya ibn Zakariya (peace be upon them). *Moa'mer narrated:* Children told Yahya ibn Zakariya (peace be upon them): come with us to play. He said: we were created to play?! *Wahb ibn Monabbah narrated:* a

Asceticism - Part 1 -

caller from Heaven called that Yahya ibn Zakaria (peace be upon them) is the master of all creatures and that Georgis is the master of martyrs". ***Yahya ibn Ja'dahah narrated*** that the Prophet (peace be upon him) said: Yahya ibn Zakariya did not commit a sin and did not scratch a woman in his chest". ***Abdullah ibn Omar narrated:*** the most beloved to God is strangers. He said, it was said: Who are the strangers? He said: who are fleeing with their religion and gathered with with Jesus ibn of Maryam (peace be upon him) on the Day of Resurrection". ***Mohamed ibn Soqa narrated:*** Jesus ibn Maryam (peace be upon him) said: "Let the people be comforted from you in peace, and let your soul be occupied in work. Let them and do not seek their blessings, or win their sins, and do what you intended to do". ***Ibn Abbas narrated:*** God, Almighty revealed to Jesus (peace be upon him): consider me part of yourself as your grieve, make me munition to your enemies, and put your trust in me so I will protect you, and do not follow other than me so not to let you down". ***Al Sha'eby narrated:*** Jesus (peace be upon him) said: Charity is not to be good to those who did good to you, but the charity is be good to those who offended you". ***Thabet narrated:*** Jesus (peace be upon him) went to visit a brother and he met a man who said to him: your brother died, so he returned and the daughters of his brother heard that he returned, so they went to him and told him:

"O Messenger of Allah, your return is more severe to us than the death of our father. And they went out to show him his grave, and he said, he screamed and went out with gray-hair, then said: Are you so? He said: Yes, he said: What do I see in you?! He said: I heard your voice, but I though it's The Scream. He said: and his wife sees and hears what he did: "Blessed is the belly you stayed in, and breasts that you fed from. Jesus said: Blessed is the one who God Almighty taught him his book, and then did not die mighty!

" *Al Hassan narrated:* Jesus ibn Maryam (peace be upon him) said: I dropped earth on its face and sat on its back, and I have not a child to die, nor a house to be destroyed. ! They said to him: Do not you take a home for you? He said: built me on the path of the torrent of the house, they said: do not prove they said to him! He said: built me a house on the path of the torrent". They said: do not prove they said: Do not take you a wife? ! He said: What do I make with a dying wife? ! *Ga'afar ibn Jerfas narrated:* Jesus ibn Maryam (peace be upon him) said: The top of sin is the love of the world, the women of creel of the Devil, and wine is the key to all evil". *Sophian narrated:* Jesus ibn Maryam (peace be upon him) said: "The love of the world is the source of all sin. Money has a lot of sickness." They said: "What is its sickness?" He said: "its owner is afflicted by pride and arrogance". They said: what If he is not afflicted? He said: His

desire to reform takes him away from the remembrance of God".
Wahab ibn Monabbah narrated: Jesus son of Maryam said: I truly say to you: The sky is free of the rich and to enter camel in the pore of the tailor easier than entering the rich into paradise".
Ibn Hoashab narrated: Jesus ibn Maryam said to the apostles: "As kings have left wisdom to you and, leave the world to them". **Wahab ibn Monabbah narrated:** The table was brought down with a pinch of barley and meat". **Akrama narrated:** Jesus ibn Maryam (peace be upon him) said to the Apostles: "O Apostles, do not give the pearls of the pig; it will not do anything with it, nor give wisdom to those who do not want it; wisdom is better than pearls; who does not want it is worse than a pic". **Sophian narrated:** Jesus ibn Maryam (peace be upon him) said to the readers: "O salt of the earth, do not be spoiled, if something is spoiled, it will only be repaired by salt. If salt is spoiled, nothing will fix it*".* **Zar'a ibn Ibrahem narrated:** Jesus ibn Maryam, peace be upon him, says: "I really say to you right: as none of you can build a house on the waves of the sea, so is the world do not take it as a decision". **Maysara narrated:** Jesus (peace be upon him) said: "If you would like to be righteous to Allah Almighty and the light of the sons of Adam from His creation, then exhale those who have wronged you, ask for those who do not ask for you, do good to those who do not do good to you, and lend those who do not reward you*".* **Sa'ed ibn Abdel**

Aziz narrated about his senators: Jesus peace be upon him passed on Akif road with a man of his apostles when a man stopped them and said: "I will not let you go until I slap you". They tried to convince him not to do that, but he refused. Jesus said: this is my cheek, slap it. He said: he slapped him and let him go. He said to apostle: "I will not let you go until I slap you". He refused. When Jesus (peace be upon him) saw this, he gave him his other cheek, so he slapped him and let him go. He said, "O God, if this is for your satisfaction, let me reach your satisfied, and if it's a scoundrel, then you are more adequate to jealousy". ***Abdullah ibn Dinar Al-Bohrany narrated:*** Jesus (peace be upon him) said to apostles: You have to bake barley and get out of this world safe and secured. Truly, I say to you: that who did the worst work is who loves the world and prefers it than his work! if he wish, he will make all the people do same work like him. Truly, I say to you: The bitterness of this world is the sweetness of the Hereafter, and the worshipers of Allah are not blessed". ***Sophian narrated:*** Jesus ibn Maryam (peace be upon him), said, "I speak to you to learn, and I will not speak to you to wonder." Yahya said, "I do not speak to you". ***Sa'eed ibn Abdelaziz narrated:*** Jesus ibn Maryam (peace be upon him) was talking to God, Almighty: it's not as I want but as you want and not as I like but as you like". ***Sa'eed ibn Abdelaziz narrated***: I was informed that no word was said to Jesus ibn Maryam (peace be upon him) was most beloved to him than to be said: This was a poor man". ***Abo Halis narrated:*** apostles said: O Christ of God, see how it is beautiful the house of God! He said: Amen Amen! Indeed, I say to you: God does not leave from this mosque a stone built on a stone , but destroyed by the sins of its family. God does not make anything with such gold or silver or stones. The good hearts are the most beloved to God, including, with them God builds the land and destroys the land if it is otherwise". ***Abo Halis narrated:*** Jesus ibn Maryam (peace be upon him) said: The devil is with the world, his cheat is with money, his decoration is with fancy and its completion is with desires". ***Al Mohajer ibn Habib narrated:*** Jesus Christ, the Son of Maryam, peace be upon him, used to say: "O group of Apostles, do not ask for the world with destroying yourselves, and ask for yourselves by leaving what is inside it. You come naked and go naked. Do not ask for tomorrow's provisions, today is enough for the day. Tomorrow will come with its work. And ask God to make your livelihood day by day. "***Ja'far ibn Barqan narrated:*** Jesus ibn Maryam (peace be upon him) said: Oh God, I have become dependent on my work and there is no poor poorer than me". ***Ja'far Al-Khory narrated:*** O God, I have become unable to push away what I hate, I do not have the benefit of what I hope, it became a matter of others. I have become dependent on my work and there is no poor poorer than me. Do not make my enemy gloat over my grief, don't make my friend hurt me, do not make my calamity in my religion and do not empower on me who does not have mercy ". ***Moslem ibn Abo Al Ja'ad narrated:*** A man from Saleh nation (peace be upon him) had offended them, they said, "O Prophet of God, pray to Allah against him, he said: Go, you have been protected." He said: "He went out every day to be cut down trees." He said: "one day, he went out with two loafs, He said: "He ate one and give charity with the other". He said: He cut down trees and came back safely. He said: Salih (peace be upon him) came with his trees safely with no harm". He said:" Salih (peace be upon him) called him and said: What did you do today? "He said: I went out with two loafs, I gave charity with one of them and ate the other". Salih said: untie your trees. He untied his trees. It has black branch on a stump of the trees. "he said:" He used it to pay for charity". ***Mousa Al-Aswary narrated:*** God Almighty revealed to a prophet of the Bani Israel (peace be upon them): All the sons of Adam are sinners, and the best sinners are the repentant". ***Khaled ibn Thabet Al-Rob'y narrated:*** I was informed that there was a young man in the Bani Israel who had read the Book and taught it. He was unknown between them, and he asked for his knowledge and his reading honor and money, and that he invented heresies. He got honor and money in the world. He lived until he reached old

Asceticism - Part 1 -

age. One night, while he was sleeping on his bed, thinking to himself, he said: these people do not know what I was invented, Doesn't God Almighty know what I invented and the death time approached? If it comes, I will seek forgiveness". He said:" he reached in his diligence in repentance that he punched his collar-bone, made a chain in it, then fixed it to the ceiling of the mosque". then he said: I will not leave my place until God grants me repentance or I die". He said: He did not deny the revelation in Bani Israel so God Almighty revealed with his situation to one of the prophets: If you committed a sin between Me and you, I will forgive you no matter how big it is. How some of my servants get lost, and when they die, I repent to them, then I put them in hell, so I do not repent to you. Auf said: I thought it is said: his was called: Berberian". **Wahb ibn Monnabah narrated:** A woman from Bani Israel passed by water, she washed herself then she prayed. She stayed sixty years or seventy years and did not leave, did not eat or drink until she gave charity, then she left. It was said to her: How were you? She said, "when I wake up, I thought I will die at night, and when I sleep, I thought I will not wake up". **Wahb ibn Monnabah narrated:** A scholar of Bani Israel came to a scholar above him in knowledge, and he said: What shall I eat? He said: "What will extinguish your hunger, he said: What shall I wear? He said: What hides your body or said: The clothing of Jesus) peace be upon him)He said: What shall I build? He said: "What hides you from the sun and protects you from the wind". He said, "How much shall I laugh?" He said: What twinkles your face. He said: How much shall I cry? He said: Do not get bored of the cry from fear of Allah Almighty". He said: What shall I show of my work? He said: What is followed by the week and makes people believe you". He said: What shall I conceal of my work? He said: What might be thought as you do not do good".

Wahb ibn Monnabah narrated: A slave of Bani Israel worshiped and swore until his hair became thick. He covered his vagina. A man died who has no other heir except him, and they refused to take his money without notifying him, so they sit by him. When he looked at them, he ran away from them. A man said: if you made me something, I will get you his news. They made something for him. He sit by him, when he saw him, he welcomed him and threw his cloths When he looked at him, he stood up and hid his eyes, he said to him: "let me come close to you". He said: come close to me". He said: A man died and left money and did not leave any other heir except you, so they refused to take money without notifying you". He said: How much he had since he died?". He said: so and so". He said: How much do I have since I left you? He said: so and so". He said: I have come before him with so and so. Then he turned and left.

Malik ibn Dinar narrated: It was said to Bani Israel: You call

Asceticism - Part 1 -

with your tongues and your hearts are far from me, void of what you fear*"*. ***Some of the elders narrated:*** Soliman ibn Abdel Malik entered the Damascus mosque and saw a stone inscription. He said: What is this? They said: we don't know". It was said: O Commander of the faithful Send to Wahab ibn Monabbah as he reads all books. The, he sent him and he knew the Book and read it, it says: "the son of Adam, if you saw what remained for you, you will be less inclined towards how long you want your hope to be, but received your regret, you foot stumbled, left by your beloved and your family. You will not return to your family, nor you add to your work. Work for the Day of Resurrection before the grief and the regret". ***Malik ibn Dinar narrated:*** Bani Israel entered a mosque for them on the day of Eid. A young boy stood at the door of the mosque from outside, so he began to cry and raise his voice in tears. He said to himself, "Not someone like me enters with you, I am a friend of so and so. It became written on the tongue of one of their prophets that someone from the righteous for that boy". ***Wahab ibn Monabbah narrated:*** It is found in some books of the prophets peace be upon them that Allah, Almighty says: Who used the money of the poor, I punish him with poverty, and if a house is built with the strength of the weak, I will ruin it". Shak Abo Mohamed narrated: a slave from Bani Israel was in the silo worshiping when someone said: If we take away anything from him! They went to a woman of sin and said to her: "expose to him." He said: she went to him in a rainy dark night. She said: "O servant of Allah, keep me inside, while he is standing to pray, and his lamp is piercing, he did not look at her. She said: "O servant of Allah, darkness and rain, keep me inside". He said: He brought her inside, so she slept on bed when he is about to pray. She moved around to show him her beauty, until his soul called him at her. He said: "By Allah no, until I know how much I can hold the fire. He came close to the lamp and put his finger in it until it burns." Then he went back to the prayer hall and his soul called him at her. He returned to the lamp and also put his finger until it burned. "He said:" Then he went back to the prayer hall and his soul called him at her too, and he returned to the lamp until his fingers were burned and she looked at him, got shocked and died. "Then he said," When they woke up they went to see what she did. He said: she is dead. He said: They said "O enemy of God, the hypocrite, you killed her, "he said:" They brought him to their king and testified against him, he ordered to Kill him! He said: "let me pray two rak'ahs." He said: "He prayed and then he invokes and said: 'Lord, I know that you would not have taken me for what I did not do, but I ask you not to be a reproach to my readers after me". God Almighty returned her soul to her. She said: Look at his hand and then returned dead ". **Wahb ibn Monabbah narrated:** He said: A man from the tourists was in a house near a village, he said: she said when I saw his hands burned, I was shocked in my place. then she said: Go away, I am not your friend all my life, so she went in the mountains". *Wahab narrated:* A tourist and his helper passed by a lion while it is on the road seeking prey. The helper said to the tourist: Lion Lion! the tourist did not pay attention to it until they passed by the lion, so the lion stepped aside from the road. When they passed, the helper told the tourist: didn't I warn you from the lion?! The tourist said: Did you think I fear anything but God Almighty?! Tongues might differ, I would love the most that God knows I fear nothing but him". *Wahab narrated:* A tourist and his helper received food once every three days, when one of them did not get his food, the elder said to his helper: One of us has done something that prevented his provision. Remember what you did. The helper said, "I did not do anything." Then the helper said: Yes, a poor man came to the door and I closed the door in his face, and he said: "Then we came and begged Allah Almighty, and their provision came as it came before". *Monther ibn Monabbah narrated:* A tourist entered a village and a man of the great people of that village died. He went out of it and said: "I do not bury this mighty man, and then he sleeps." Then a man came and said: "O man, do you have any mercy from Allah?" He said: No, until he said that three times, and he said, "He does not say, and how do you know what happened in his suffering". ***Wahab narrated:*** there were a tourist with his helper, the tourist said to his helper: enter the village and buy for me a cerement, I am dead. The helper entered and there was a great person from the village has died and people rallied in burying him, they closed their shops so the helper could not afford it until he returned and bought a cerement and wheat. He returned to his friend who has died, and the lion ate his face. He grieved and bowed. He said: "This mighty man was put in cerement, embalmed, and buried, while this man the lion ate his face. It was he said: "As for this mighty man, he had not even a single good deed. Allah Almighty wanted to take him out from this world and he has no share in the Hereafter. As for this tourist man, he did a small work so that work so that God took him out of the world and he did not find the pain in that". ***Wahab narrated:*** A tourist was sent with a king, the king ordered to do whatever the tourist did, "he said." They entered a valley and saw a cadaver. Then the tourist covered his nose with his cloth from the smell of the cadaver and the king did as the tourist did. The tourist said to him: why did you do that? He said: I was ordered to do as you do, the tourist said to him: " have you found a wind as I have found?" The king said, "Nothing harms us except the smell of the unbelievers". ***Wahab narrated:*** The man was on the hearth of the House of Jerusalem and had two sons. When they become

Asceticism - Part 1 -

mature, they tampered with women and it was not denied for them, God Almighty said: By my dignity, I will kill them all three of them in one day, and I will empower poverty on their family after their death". the people of Oman after poverty". Wahab narrated: The devil - cursed by God - came to a tourist, he asked his help, then he did not get anything from him. He said to him: I want to be your friend. The tourist said: I do not need your friendship. He said: if you ask me anything, I will tell you said: He said: Yes. He said: How you seduce people?". He said: "We look at those who are in a hurry and sharp and we play by them as boys play with the balls". *Wahab ibn Monabbah narrated:* Some of Bani Israel Rabbis said: I became like a tramp of the picker, and like the spike of the stern, he said: how much shall I be pious to God! *Wahab ibn Monabbah narrated:* There appeared in Bani Israel vicious readers, and they will multiply in you". *Malik ibn Dinar narrated:* God revealed to a prophet of the prophets of Bani Israel: Say to your people not to eat the food of my enemies, not to drink the drink of my enemies, and not to appear like my enemies, then they will be my enemies as they are my enemies". Malik ibn Dinar narrated: The house of one of Bani Israel rabbis was filled with men and women, he was preaching them and reminding them of the days of God. He said: he saw one of his sons one day winking to women, then he said: Hey son! "He said:" He fell from his bed, lost his burden, dropped his wife and killed his sons in the army. God inspired to their prophet to tell your friend the rabbi that I will never get out of your crucifix as a friend, your anger with me because I said: Hey son! Hey son! **Malik ibn Dinar narrated:** It is written in the Torah: "Whoever has a neighbor who commits sin, and not forbidding him to do, then he is his partner". **Malik ibn Anas narrated:** I was informed that a group of Bani Israel fast the day, and if the night comes and the food are made, they will make it an episode among them. A man stands and say to them, "Do not eat too much, then drink too much, then sleep too much". **Wahab ibn Monabbah narrated**: Jermiah said: O Lord, you have chosen your servant Dawood (peace be upon him) to build a mosque for you, and you raised him so much until he was like a pride empowered on him from his troop. He said: it was said to him: you see, if you are told about crunch of the sun or a measure of the wind or the response of tomorrow, Or you are told: Do you know how many doors for the sky? How many storages for God Almighty? Or how many fountains in the sea? Or you find the sea quarrels with the land". The sea told you: I have multiplied in my waves, and my fountains have multiplied, and I wanted to lean on the land. The land said to you: I have multiplied in my trees, and multiplied in mountains, and multiplied in my wolves, and multiplied in rivers. I wanted to lean on the sea for which you

Asceticism - Part 1 -

set forth?" ***Abo Al-Jalad narrated:*** I read in Wisdom: Whoever has preacher in himself, God will be his protector, and who is fair to people in himself, God increases his dignity. Humiliation in obedience to God is closer than be gloried by sin. ***Sabih narrated:*** Wisdom states: O son of Adam, you beg me, and you find me in two letters: work with the best you learn and let the worst of what you learned". ***Abo Habib Al-Salamy narrated:*** I read in Wisdom: Listen to the questioner until he finishes his words and then answer him with mercy, and be for the orphan like the merciful father, and be a champion for the oppressor, so you might be the successor of God in his land". ***Hisham ibn Orwa narrated about his father:*** It is written in the Wisdom: "Do not betray the traitor, his betrayal is enough". ***Yazid ibn Maysara narrated:*** It is written in the Wisdom: "Allah Almighty says: O young man who abandons his lust for me, who humbles his youth for me, you are like some of my angels to me". ***Qatada narrated:*** it's written in Torah: O son of Adam, you remember me by your tongue and forget me, you call me and escape from me, and I give you provision and you worship others! .

ABOUT THE AUTHOR

The Imam Aḥmad ibn Ḥanbal, (born 780, Baghdad—died 855, Baghdad), Muslim theologian, jurist, and one of Islam great Scholars. He was the compiler of the Traditions of the Prophet Mohammad PBUH in the Musnad and formulator of the Ḥanbali Fqih School, one of the four main Islamic schools of jurisdiction.

www.ingramcontent.com/pod-product-compliance
Lightning Source LLC
Chambersburg PA
CBHW022131160426
43197CB00009B/1234